Coming Full Circle

T0162688

Coming Full Circle

Karen Lynn

Library of Congress Control Number: 2011908799
ISBN: Hardcover   978-1-4628-7941-0
                   Softcover   978-1-4628-7940-3
                   Ebook   978-1-4628-7942-7

This book was printed in the United States of America.

To order additional copies of this book, contact:
Xlibris Corporation
1-888-795-4274
www.Xlibris.com
Orders@Xlibris.com
92820

CONTENTS

This book is written in loving memory of my parents and Dave, my soul mate and younger brother, who died too young. It is dedicated to Don and all the men and women who served our country, both here and abroad, during the Vietnam years.

I am the woman I have become
because of the people I have known in my life.
K.L   2011

Chapter One
The Vietnam Years

The Protest

UNTIL WE WERE right outside of Washington, D.C., the traffic moved right along. But, the closer we had gotten to D.C., the slower and more congested the traffic was. Along the road, cars had pulled off to the side. Other cars were parked on the median strip. It looked like people had camped out all day, hoping to find the perfect spot along the Potomac. A fireworks display was scheduled for that evening. The waterways that surrounded the capital city were crowded with boats.

Because so many people were in Washington for the Persian Gulf victory celebration, cars were being turned away at one of the entrances. We had to find an alternate route to get into the district. We had no problem getting into D.C. once we switched roads.

As we drove through Washington, I saw the Vietnam Memorial from a distance. Already tears were beginning to run down my cheeks. Just seeing the Wall made me fall apart, I wiped away the tears from my face, hoping no one noticed me.

How did I get so involved with the Vietnam War? On the other hand, how could I not have been so emotionally involved? Two parts of my life, both affected by different wars, came together because of the victory in yet another war. My thoughts drifted back to a time that seemed so long ago, although emotionally, seeing the Wall made it seem like it was only yesterday . . .

Baltimore was like any other American Metropolitan city in the late 1960's—still reeling from losing a President to an assassin's bullet. People were protesting and marching everywhere and the almost daily pictures of the "Vietnam Conflict" came into our living rooms with vivid color. Vietnam was on everyone's mind.

In the spring of 1968, my girlfriend Cathy heard that there was to be an important war protest at Towson University, so we decided to skip school to join the demonstration. Towson is located one mile from where we went to high school. Located off of one of Baltimore's main roads, all activities were in front of the University where they were visible to all who passed by. Once we were a safe distance from our high school, we put on our black arm bands.

It was a beautiful, warm day. The trees were beginning to bloom and flowers were sprouting from the ground. My thoughts of things coming to life again were shattered by the thoughts of death as the protestors began to carry mock coffins that were placed before the large crowd. After they put down the coffins, a hush fell over the crowd. One man picked up the megaphone and began to speak."Our brothers and fathers are being sent home from Vietnam in flag-draped coffins and we are not stopping it. We have to stop!" he yelled at the crowd. Another man stepped forward and said, "We want peace now!" "Stop this war! Stop the baby killers'" "Peace now!" Everyone began to cheer and chant "Peace now." The crowd drowned out whoever was speaking.

I thought war was wrong and hoped for a swift end to this "conflict." I prayed for peace. At seventeen, I hated to think that young men only one year older than me were being drafted and sent to Vietnam. I never thought I could ever look at war and make any sense of it.

We stayed for most of the rally as we showed our protest of the war by wearing black arm bands representing the death that war brings. As much as I agreed with wanting the war to end, something about my being there really bothered me, the protest depressed me and I was glad to leave.

Cathy and I left together and walked down the road with our arms bands still in place. She was revved-up and excited thinking the rally would change things as we parted to go our own way home. I was walking down the road when I realized what it was that upset me and immediately took off the arm bands. Feeling ashamed of myself, I stuck them in a bush.

Baby-Killers. Did we ever call our fathers and uncles "Baby-Killers?" Did anyone ever hang all that guilt on other soldiers from another war? Did we treat them with no respect when they came home? Why start now with our brothers? Was the Vietnam War any worse than any other war?

Even if I did not support the war, there was no way I would not support those who served or would serve. Right or wrong, after what the veterans had been through over there, lack of respect was the last thing they needed.

The USO

DEMONSTRATIONS AND THE war continued. The draft seemed to be affecting everyone I knew. One of my brothers joined the National Guard to avoid being drafted, while another brother enlisted in the Navy. Although I still protested the war, I wanted to show my support for our servicemen. After high school graduation, I joined the Baltimore USO.

The USO stands for United Service Organization, or as some men called it, Uncle Sam's Orphanage or simply, the club. It was located in the heart of downtown Baltimore.

The USO was for all military personnel but except for a few special functions when officers came, we mostly saw the enlisted men. In my three years at the club, I only saw one woman who was in the military come to the USO. For an out-of-town serviceman, it was a place to socialize and get away from the ship or barracks for a while.

Often, there were movies or sports game passes for the servicemen. Except for Mrs. Shatner who was in charge of special events and the business end of the club, the chaperones and hostesses where volunteers.

The USO was a big hall with a stage in the back. Three pool tables lined the left side while a TV surrounded by comfortable arm chairs and a large sofa was on the right side. In the middle of the hall were tables and chairs which could be folded leaving plenty of room to dance.

Above the dance floor was a large disco ball. Pinball machines, a ping-pong table, a jukebox and some soda machines were along both sides of the steps leading to the entrance.

Downstairs were the restrooms and a small lounge. The reception desk was on the side in front of the stage by the table with the coffee and tea pot along with donuts and assorted snacks. The club had a warm and welcoming air about it.

To be a hostess, we had to be a high school graduate, single and have a job. I was a full-time dental assistant for my dad. We filled out a questionnaire and were then interviewed by Mrs. Shatner. We had rules to follow. One of which was to behave in a lady like manner and dress accordingly. The important part of being a hostess was to make the servicemen feel welcome and comfortable at the club. We were told to circulate with all of the men, not just the best looking ones.

Although we were not supposed to date or leave the USO after closing with the servicemen, it happened. Often a group of us would meet at a restaurant around the corner from the club to get something to eat and hang out for a while.

The Baltimore area was home to Ft. Meade Army Base, the Coast Guard base at Curtis Bay and at that time, a large Naval Yard where ships were stationed while in dry dock for repairs.

The USO held parties for special occasions, variety and movie nights, held dances and once sponsored a four day NATO conference.

Often deep friendships developed and it was hard when the guys left, especially if they were going to Vietnam. I learned to make the best of the time spent together. I hope some of the guys look back at those times with fond memories as I do.

Don

WHEN I MET Don I had just recently started working at the USO. It was a cold Sunday afternoon. "Pop" had called me and asked if I would come down to the club for awhile. There were only 2 other hostesses at the USO that day. I was playing a game of pool when Don and his friends, Dave and Paul came in.

Fresh out of boot camp, they would be heading off to Vietnam after several months of special training at Ft. Meade army base.

After my game of pool was finished, Pop called me over to the reception desk and introduced me to Don who had been asking about things to do in Baltimore. After talking at the desk for awhile, we got ourselves a tea and a donut and sat down at a quiet table and our friendship began.

Don was a tall young man, with green eyes and sandy brown hair. When he smiled, dimples appeared. He was an attractive man, I was 19 when I met Don who was 21 years old, I looked up to him.

Don loved life and lived it with enthusiasm. He was funny and very caring. A day didn't go by since we met that he didn't see me or call. Don was a kindred spirit and became one of my closest friends.

Don was one of those rare people that you meet in life that you never forget. He had a presence about him that has stayed with me.

One day after we had been to the Baltimore museum of Art, we took a walk when a light snow began to fall as we walked hand in hand. Suddenly Don turned to me and kissed me.

"I couldn't help myself" he laughed as his eyes twinkled. He suddenly became very serious and said" If I die in Vietnam, don't cry for me, I will be in a better place."

"I don't want to think about you being killed", I blurted out as tears began to run down my face.

"Death is not the end but the beginning. To fear death is to deny what we believe in."

"I don't want to go to Vietnam to leave you worrying about me. To be honest I don't want to leave you, I have tried to hide my feelings about you, but I have a job to do," he added.

Don was drafted when he was in college but believed he had a duty to serve our country just as his father and grandfather did.

"If I had not been drafted, I would not have met you."

The worst part of saying goodbye is the uncertainty of it. "Will he come back alive?" I knew this day was coming and I dreaded it. For months, I told myself not to think about it until tomorrow and tomorrow was now.

As he gave me a kiss and our last hug-goodbye, I felt it, I sensed his fate in my stomach and it was an intense sadness in my heart. And he was gone.

A few months later, I was at the club when I received word that Don, Paul and Dave, along with most of their company, were killed in Vietnam. It felt like someone ripped my heart out of my chest. Paul and Rick were giving me the bad news.

> I feel numb, this is not happening, it's a bad dream, but I am not asleep. The whole thing is a sick joke! Don is not dead. I want to stand up and hug Paul as I cry but my legs are numb and I can't stand up. People are talking but I can't hear them. Both Paul and Rick are telling me how sorry they are to be telling me this.

Paul and Rick were friends from the club. Rick was a grief therapist. Rick knew that it wasn't just the family that hurt when someone is killed. Sadly, to the military and the civilian world, Don was just another fatality in the Vietnam War.

"To say goodbye without a tear
not even blink an eye
would seem to me you never loved
a person as much as I"
Karen Derry 1969

Hair

IN THE SPRING of my sophomore year in high school, I started ushering at the Morris A. Mechanic Theatre in Baltimore. A couple of years after I began working at the theatre, the musical *Hair* made a comeback and it came to the Mechanic.

The theatre was a separate part of my life, a place where I could come to see a play, which entertained and distracted me from the realities of the world. When I entered the theatre doors, I'd leave my day at school, work, or the USO at the door.

There were the plays that hit home, that struck a nerve and made a connection with something happening in my own life; *Hair* was one of them.

The guys from the USO knew that I worked at the Mechanic and they often asked me about the latest plays I had seen. Bob, Paul, and Steve were three guys at the club who really wanted to see the play. But since they were in the army and going to Vietnam, I had reservations about taking them to see *Hair*.

Among other things, *Hair* deals with the sixties, the desires of peace and the burning of draft cards to protest Vietnam War. In the play one of the characters gets drafted, goes to Vietnam and is killed there.

I had tried to get tickets, but **Hair** was a popular show and the tickets had sold out quickly. Knowing how disappointed the guys were, I told a few friends at the theatre about our situation and they offered to get us in the theatre without tickets.

One of my friends was a head usher and he met us at the parking lot elevator. He took us up to the balcony because it was a full house. We had to stand through the entire play but no-one seemed to mind.

Many of the songs in the play were popular and it was an entertaining play. As the play ends, one of the characters is killed in the war and the sobering reality hit like a ton of bricks. The theme that ran throughout the play was that Vietnam was an unpopular war and that until it ended; too many people would continue to die.

As soon as the play ended, we left the theatre to beat the crowd. Once outside the theatre, we all lit a cigarette. The four of us began walking away from the theatre and all of them were very quiet.

"Well, what did you think of the play?" I asked.

"It was good, I liked it, but it really made me think . . . ." Steve said, not really finishing his thought.

"I can see now, why you hesitated about taking us", Bob said.

"Why?" Paul quickly asked. "We know what could happen to us in Vietnam!"

"Yeah, but who wants to think about it?" Steve said.

"My cousin was killed in 'Nam and when my mom found out I was going too, she went nuts. She was ready to drive me to Canada to stop me from going." said Bob.

"When I get back from Vietnam, I'm going to grow my hair real long", Paul said as he rubbed his crew cut.

We all laughed and it eased the tension of the subject of war. We walked to a nearby restaurant where I was their guest for dinner.

Shannon

WITH HER CARROT-COLORED hair, green eyes, freckles and her unmistakable brogue, it was obvious Shannon was from Ireland. Her smile revealed pearly white teeth with a gap in the front. In spite of the personal tragedies she had suffered in her life, Shannon was one of the happiest and funniest people I had ever met.

Shannon had come from Belfast in Northern Ireland. She was one of nine children in her Catholic family. One day while her parents, a brother and a sister had gone shopping, a bomb exploded in the shopping district killing all four of them.

Shannon had been living in Ireland at the time of the accident, so her brother in Baltimore invited Shannon to come and live with him and his wife. Wanting to start a new life and emerge from the horrors of war, she gladly accepted.

Shortly after arriving in the States, Shannon began working as a courtroom stenographer. Wanting to meet people, she heard about the U.S.O. and went there to volunteer as a hostess. Shannon was very outgoing and friendly but she kept her personal life private.

At first she always went home after the U.S.O. closed for the evening rather than going out with the group of us to get something to eat. After several weeks, we had become good friends and it was rare for her not to join us.

For a while, I thought Shannon's familiarity with different aspects of war would make it easier for her to relate to anyone who had been in a war situation. But she saw a war as having both aggressors and victims.

The IRA and American G.I.'s were the aggressors and the civilians were the victims. As a victim in Ireland's civil war, Shannon sympathized with the Vietnamese civilians.

During our one and only discussion concerning the Vietnam War, the point was made that many times it was the civilians who participated in the atrocities of war. Shannon's reply was in the form of a question; "who wouldn't do almost anything to protect their family and their home?" Shannon sympathized with the Vietnam Vets in that it was tragic that anyone had to fight in a war that was not fought on their own soil.

By the time the discussion was over, two things were evident: That War was hell, and it would be better if Shannon met men who were not directly involved with the Vietnam War.

I often thought of how if Shannon and I lived in Ireland, our friendship would be complicated by the fact that she was a Catholic and I was a Protestant. Even my British lineage that was equally divided between my Irish grandfather and my English grandmother would be a factor.

We never discussed politics and when we talked about our faith it was only common, basic, Christian beliefs. Religion was the central part of both of our lives along with our family and friends.

Eventually, Shannon met and became involved with a guy she met at work and we drifted apart. I often thought of Shannon and I still miss her ability to make me laugh in spite of life's problems.

Paul

PAUL WAS ONE of the first people I had met at the USO and we became close friends. Paul was an attractive man. Tall with a stocky build and big brown eyes; his thick black hair and a mustache reflected his Italian heritage. Paul seemed a lot older than his 22 years.

Paul had been to Vietnam twice. He was drafted for his first tour and at first objected to going to Vietnam just for the sake of killing. He could agree with going to Vietnam to ensure peace in the country, but he knew that wasn't the case. Being in the army's infantry division, he saw a lot of good men die.

He came home very angry that so many innocent people had to die, and for what? He also came home to a wife that found comfort with another man while he was away. Bitter, he signed up for another tour.

Paul was promoted during his second tour; giving him more responsibility to the men he served with. Paul never talked much about the actual fighting, but he did say that if you waited until you saw the white's of their eyes, it was too late. To stay alive, you had to be the aggressor.

Paul was quiet and kept to himself. Often I would look over at him and he would have a look in his eyes that looked like both fear and anger. Almost as if he was in a trance, he looked like his thoughts were far away. It was the look that many vets called the "stare."

Paul's constant companion was his guitar. Often, Paul would sit in the lounge downstairs singing for hours as he played his guitar. His singing had a professional quality to it and as he sang, his guitar complimented the songs.

Sometimes his songs were reflections of the pain he was going through. I often sat close to the stairs that led to the downstairs lounge to hear him sing. Once he heard me singing to a familiar song and he asked me to join him. We began singing together.

What made Paul and I close friends was the fact that we were always there for each other, whether it was a quiet walk under a large umbrella on a rainy day or enjoying a funny movie when we needed to laugh.

Paul had known Don and when he had heard about his death, Paul had come down to the USO from Fort Meade so I wouldn't be alone when I heard about Don's death.

Paul was with me when two other mutual friends told me the terrible news and I was thankful I had Paul to lean on. When Paul's divorce was final I made sure I was there for him. Paul experienced many mood swings; he must have felt as if his life was one big roller-coaster ride.

He went to Vietnam a happily married, peace-loving guy who wanted to raise a family and he came back a bitter, divorced vet who felt that peace and happily-ever-after only existed in fairy tales.

Paul began opening up to other Vietnam vets and together they were a support group to each other. Knowing others had experienced the same feelings and nightmares, Paul felt better knowing he wasn't alone. In time, Paul became a happier man and the songs he sang were those of hope and promise.

The Korean Vet

IT WOULD BE hard not to notice him as he paced back and forth never losing steps. He walked from one end of the hall to the other, clicking his heels as he turned around. He walked his post hour after hour keeping watch. Occasionally, he would sit down to watch TV and rest as he took a coffee break. He never left his post for long.

Tall and trim, he appeared to be in his mid-forties. His blond hair was kept trimmed in a military cut. His eyes were piercing gray and when he looked at anyone, it was as if he was looking right through them. A glance from him would send chills up my spine. With his strong chin and masculine features, he could be considered handsome if he didn't have such a cold, stone-faced appearance.

Every so often, he would shout out orders, then run and duck behind one of the columns in the club as if he was under fire. His moves were so mechanical he acted like a programmed robot. A veteran of the Korean War, he had suffered from shell shock. He seemed destined to spend the rest of his life reliving the war and fighting the enemy in a war that only continued to exist in his mind.

The first time I saw him at the USO, he was walking back and forth when he suddenly shouted out that there was incoming mortar and ran for cover.

When he felt he was out of danger, he resumed his pacing as he cuddled his rifle that was never there.

Although he seemed unaware of what was going on around him, there were those rare times when something brought him back to reality. He would be polite, but he would limit the conversation to weather or comment on a television show someone was watching.

When it was time for the USO to close for the evening, he would walk away as if he knew just where he was going. The chaperones said he had a room at the VA hospital. As far as anyone knew, he had no family. He was a reminder of the affect a war could have on anyone who had to experience the horrors of war.

A Soldier's Story

WE HAD NEVER met before. We had been brought together by a mutual friend who arranged our meeting. Having just gotten back from Vietnam, he had needed to talk to someone who wouldn't analyze or question his actions during his tour. He preferred to talk to someone he wouldn't see again.

We met at the Trailways' bus station in downtown Baltimore, not far from the USO. The coffee shop was open all night and I was off the next day so we didn't have to worry about time. He had been having a hard time sleeping since the war, so it didn't bother him to stay up late.

He bought me a cup of tea and a coffee for himself. I followed his lead as he walked over to a corner table away from the clatter of dishes, the noise of the cash register and other people.

There was no need for a big introduction. After five minutes of small talk, he told me his story.

His unit was sent as relief for another unit that had been hit hard. There were many casualties and fatalities. Before his unit boarded the helicopter, he knew it would be bad. When he arrived at his destination, wounded American soldiers were everywhere. Gunfire, explosions and men screaming in pain accompanied his every thought. "I came here for this?"

He passed a corpsman who had done all he could for a dying U.S. soldier, but the soldier was so shot up, he never had a chance. He felt sick and he was scared. All he wanted to do was run and hide. He had been trained for combat, but nothing had prepared him for what he saw. He ran into the thick bush of the country. "Which way should I go?" he asked himself.

His buddy followed him. Gunfire was getting closer. He looked to see what was going on around him. He turned his head and saw his buddy's head being blown away. Immobilized by fear, he was unable to scream or move. Someone shouted to him to keep moving. His fear was replaced by anger and he went charging through the woods shooting his rifle at the running Viet Cong in the distance ahead. In revenge, he shot every gook that he could during the remainder of his tour. He had become a killer. He felt a lot of remorse, but he also felt that he had done the job he was trained to do.

At times, his lip quivered as he told of his experience. It was obvious that he was trying to hold back his emotions to finish his story. By the time he was finished, we both had tears in our eyes. We sat there in awkward silence as he pulled himself together. I didn't know what to say, so I said nothing.

He got up to get us another drink and sweet rolls. He said he felt better by getting it off his chest and thanked me for listening. We soon left the bus station and he walked me back to my car. I never did see him again. But a friend of his stopped in at the USO one night. He mentioned his friend was out of the service and was doing his best to put his war experience behind him.

Troy

AFTER THREE TOURS in Vietnam, Troy was finally coming home to start a new life. A big celebration had been planned for his return. My brother, a boyhood friend, had kept in touch with him over the years. Troy was our nearest neighbor when we stayed in the country.

Growing up together, my brothers, Troy and I, explored the woods and stream looking for hidden caves between the steep hills and rocks. Together we built rope bridges between trees, a thirteen floor tree-house (never mind that at least two floors were only big enough to stand on) and helped my dad build a cabin and deck.

He was my first big crush and oh, he seemed so handsome and grown-up. But to him, I was only his friend's kid sister.

At the airport he was greeted by two of his old high school friends. After picking Troy up, the three of them stopped off to have a few drinks. Shortly after leaving the bar, the driver apparently lost control of the car and it ran off the road into some trees.

Troy and the driver were killed instantly, while his friend in the back seat was in serious condition. The policeman found the car only hours after Troy had safely landed in the States.

After all the years of worrying about their son in Vietnam, it was a cruel twist of fate to find out he was killed while driving home. But then, young men don't just die in wars. Troy was 23 years old.

The Biker/A Composite Sketch

H E POKED THE fire with the large stick he had used to roll the log closer to the red coals. Sparks rose from the fire as burning embers filtered upward slowly burning out. He poked the log one final time with the stick and carefully put it down beside him. It was a great campfire, although for a June evening we thought it might be too warm for one. But, there was always something special about friends gathering around such a fire.

He reached into his boot and pulled out his flask in which he kept his Jack Daniels and made a toast "To the good times!"

"To good people," Harry added

"The best," he added, as he looked at me from across the fire. The fire's reflection was dancing in his blue eyes. I got up from the bench I was sitting on to sit next to my handsome man.

"How'd it ride, man?" Harry asked.

"Great," he said, as he went on to talk about the ride. Hours earlier, he and I had ridden on his bike out here to wooden countryside of Pennsylvania where my parents had bought some land years ago. He and his friends needed to get away, so we came here.

As we rode his bike and hit a long stretch of open country road, he put his body down real low on the bike so I could feel the wind and pressure of the open road. Debbie and Mark had followed us in her car as Harry and Bob followed in Harry's car.

As much as I liked riding his bike with him, bikes scared me as much as they thrilled me.

Brian had a Harley Davidson. When you're standing beside a Harley with its engine running, the ground around you seems to shake. The power of the bike feels like a kind of thunder as you ride it. As they talked about bikes for awhile, my thoughts drifted off.

Remember the first time we met? I was at the U.S.O. when you walked through the front door, cold, wet and hungry. The icy rain had turned to snow and you were on your Harley. You had recently gotten back from Vietnam and you were being transferred to the Baltimore area. You had a few days before you had to report in. I had been walking toward the downstairs steps when I saw you standing by the door. I wasn't aware it was getting so bad outside.

"Looks bad out there," I said, changing my direction and walking up the steps to the door to get a better look. "Is that you're bike?" I asked, although, looking at you, it was obvious. You were wearing your leather jacket, holding your helmet and you had the same well worn boots you are wearing now.

"You're going to have to get it off the street, man, you're not going anywhere on a bike," one of the guys said. A few of the guys and I grabbed our coats and we all went outside to take a look at the snow and your bike. You lit a cigarette and I saw your hand shaking as you gripped your handlebar.

Some of the guys from the club helped you move your bike to the parking lot behind the USO. You had no other choice but to leave it there.
We all went back into the club and I brought you some hot coffee and donuts as you were trying to dry off and warm up. You were stuck with no place to go and no way to get there. You were having a bad day and I felt bad for you.

We talked for the next few hours. The chaperones closed the club early.
On an impulse, I invited you over to my apartment. It was a good thing because you ended up driving my car since you were used to driving in the snow.

On the way to my apartment, we stopped at the food store. With what money you had, you bought some food and we ended up being snowbound for two days! My dad called that evening telling me not to go to work the next day. We spent the night talking and you were a gentleman. When we finally got to your bike, it was still there with the snow on it.

"Karen, Karen? Are you still with us?" Harry interrupted my thoughts as he passed me the flask and I took a small sip and passed it. Brian put another log on the fire, lit a cigarette and put his strong arm around me. I could tell by the way his body felt, that he was relaxed. No one was going anywhere tonight.

Once I caught Brian crying over an opened Bible. I sat down next to him and put my arms around him as he cried. In Vietnam he had a hard time with the commandment, "Thou shall not kill." We would search the Bible until we found verses that brought him some comfort. To me, tears are not a sign of weakness, but a sign of pain and emotion.

The fire was hot and we had to move our benches back. Rob had gone to the car to get beer and passed one to everyone. Harry started to talk about a trip he was hoping to make and I thought about last fall.

Remember when we were in New England? Your family lived in Maine and I flew to Boston to meet you. We traveled thru New England on your bike. One day it started to rain and we stopped until the rain let up a little. As we continued up the mountain, it began to snow softly at first, then harder and it began to stick to the roads. We were lucky that we weren't very far from the motel where we made our reservation. I was frozen by the time I reached the top, but it was worth it. The view was spectacular. I wasn't sure which was more beautiful, the scenery or you.

Brian started yawning and talking about going to bed. "Karen and I are sleeping by the fire tonight," he said. The stars were bright, the moon was full and the fire would keep us from getting chilly. I went inside to get the sleeping bags, blankets, and pillows. I made a cup of tea and grabbed the tin of homemade cookies I had made.

"Holding out on me, huh?" he said smiling as he took a cookie. He passed the tin to Harry. I put the sleeping bags down under the trees, a safe distance from the fire. Harry and Bob said goodnight and went into the cabin and joined Mark and Debbie.

As I lay down next to Brian, he put his arms around me and we looked at the stars in the sky as we held one another. I drifted off to sleep in his arms. I wasn't asleep long when something woke me up. The last log Brian had put on was still burning. Then I turned to him. "Oh no!" I thought to myself, "not now!" His eyebrows were gathered together and he was sweating. Brian fitfully moved about until he woke up with a start. Sitting up on the sleeping bag, his eyes met mine. In his eyes was the lost look called the "stare". "Oh God, why?" "Hasn't he been through enough?"

Then he told me he had a reoccurring dream of something he had experienced during his tour in Nam. Brian's unit was heading towards a village when they were attacked by sniper fire. Two other men close to Brian were shot. Brian was shot in the leg. Everyone dropped to the ground to avoid getting shot. The shooting stopped and three villagers were seen running away. The men got off the ground and were relieved to find that no one had been killed. Carefully, they began to search the small village as the medic helped the wounded soldiers. The village was deserted. Nothing appeared to have been taken by the villagers; bedding, clothing and cooking utensils were left behind. A fire used for cooking food was still warm and smoldering.
A kettle of food had been set aside, indicating they had planned to get it later. Someone must have seen the unit coming and warned the other villagers.

The unit was almost finished their search when one of the men heard the muffled sound of a baby crying. The soldier went into the hut and came out carrying an infant in his arms. The soldier had only taken a few steps when the baby exploded instantly. The explosion then set the shack on fire.

He gently kissed me and then got up to sit by the campfire, putting on another log. I wrapped a blanket around us and we sat on the bench by the fire until the sun came up.

The morning was beautiful. The sun filtered through the trees and the birds were calling out to each other. Bob came outside and insisted we cook breakfast on the fire. The smell of coffee and bacon filled the air and all of us had a great breakfast before we took a hike to a nearby stream. After we finished cleaning up our mess from breakfast, we all walked down the path leading to the stream.

The path led us to a big rock we called the overlook. When one was on the rock, one could look down on the stream below. We all sat on the rock looking at the beauty around us, and then we began to make our way down to the stream. The sun made the water sparkle as it danced between the rocks.

I was stepping on the stones to get to the other side when Brian slipped into the water. I laughed so hard, I almost lost my balance. I held out my hand to help him up when he pulled me into the water. Still laughing, the others got into the water one by one.

I got out of the water to look at my biker. He and his friends were still in the stream with their clothes on, splashing each other. They reminded me of children playing. Maybe it's never too late to re-capture some of the joys of childhood.

As they got out of the water to dry off, they laughed about different things they did as kids. I was glad to see Brian so happy. We all sat on the rocks until our clothes had dried off a little before we began the climb back to the cabin.

Since it was such a beautiful day, he had decided to go for a ride on his bike. Leaving the others to entertain themselves, we took a road off the beaten path just to see where it would take us. We passed a lovely old farmhouse with a wooden porch that wrapped around it.

Quilts and blankets blew in the slight breeze while drying on the line. There was a stream running through the back yard. Sheep grazed on the sides of the stream. The dogs barked as we rode by.

The winding road took us up and down, twisting around the tree lined lane and across two bridges. When we came to the end of the road, we stopped at the corner gas station to fill up the bike. Brain bought us each a bottle of coke from the machine and then he sat down next to me on the curb by the bike. From a distance, dark clouds could be seen moving quickly across the clear sky.

"It looks like it's going to rain," I said. "Maybe we should head back before we get caught in it."

He looked at me and sighed, "I just don't feel like getting up."

The wind was beginning to pick up, so he finished his coke and went to start up the bike. He had tried to kick start it when the pedal kicked back, slamming against his right leg.

"Ah!" Brian moaned as he grabbed his leg. He remained sitting on the bike for a few minutes until the pain eased up. He tried again and got the bike started.

"How's your leg?" I asked, as I hopped on the bike.

"It's Ok", he said, rubbing it one final time.

We drove back with the wind blowing behind us, almost pushing us along the road. We were coming up the driveway when the rain hit fast and hard. Everyone was still outside sitting around the campfire. With all the trees around, no one had seen the storm moving in. We all made a dash for the cabin, hoping to avoid being drenched by the cold rain.

"Man, the wind and rain were right behind us the whole ride back," he said as the rain dripped from his dark brown hair.

Oh, I loved him! Brian was the handsome man of my dreams and I was totally in awe of him.

Remember the night when you surprised me at the club? By our reaction to seeing each other, it was obvious to everyone why we dated no one else.

"What's wrong with your leg, an old war injury?" Harry asked, obviously noticing his slight limp.

"I hurt it while I was starting up the bike. I've been having problems with that lately", he said.

"We'll take a look at the bike in the morning," Mark added.

Brian sat down next to me handing me a coke.

Harry was the first one to tell me about your leg. He said he was only a few feet away from you when you were shot. Harry had said that your leg wound was severe but that you endured two operations, pain, infection, and therapy, to keep it.

I remember the first time I saw your badly scarred leg; we were alone on the beach, watching the sunrise. The water was warm and you decided you wanted to go into the ocean for a swim. You put on cut-offs and once in the water, you forgot about any scars.

The evening went fast. We all stayed in the cabin that night due to the rain. After working on the bike the next morning, we headed back to Baltimore.

Our years together flew by too fast. But, until he could find peace with himself, he could never settle down. Oh God, it hurt when he left! I tried to console myself with the fact that I hadn't gotten burned, I just let go.

Maybe that's the hardest love of all; to love someone enough to just let go. Brian's love and presence left a big void in my life. He needed to find that open road and ride the thunder. In my heart, I know he found it and I wish him peace.

To Set the Record Straight

JOE TOLD ME that people don't understand and that broke my heart. "When I left for Vietnam for what was to be my first of two tours, I felt like some kind of hero. Everyone was buying me drinks and making me feel very special. After coming home from "Nam", I was literally spit on and cursed at. I couldn't believe the difference in how people treated me."

"During my tour, I saw some nasty things I don't even want to talk about. But there were some instances that both disgusted me and turned me off, because Americans got the bad rap. The Viet Cong would find a "friendly village" with families, including parents and children. The Viet Cong would then kill everyone in the village, bury them in a mass grave and move in.

The Americans were forbidden to shoot the civilians so as we entered friendly territory, we would be ambushed. This happened several times and many men were lost. The Viet Cong were very sneaky about attacking us. After this happened several times, I was very paranoid about entering a village."

"One night as we crept toward a village, I heard the rustling of bushes. The bushes rustled again and I was certain it was a spy looking out for us. So, I fired a round into the bushes. Feeling safe that whoever was there was dead, I went to look.

I had shot a water buffalo and for that, I was eventually fined $250. Crazy! There was never a fine for taking another life! There is no glory in killing and in war, there are no rules."

"For my second tour of duty, I was offered a post behind a desk in a small mid-western town or a tour on an unarmed ship off the coast of Vietnam. My job was to assist flying in soldiers who had been shot.

We would fly them onto the ship by helicopters, and contact their families back home. Many times it was the first contact they had with one another in months. We would stabilize the wounded men, get them to a MASH unit or hospital, or send them home."

"As an amateur radio enthusiast, I was the one responsible for getting in touch with the families back home. One thing that was never mentioned was that we would often air lift Vietnamese civilians who had been shot and treat them.

They were innocent victims and they were given good care and compassion. When they had healed or we had done the best we could for them, we took them back to their own villages.

We didn't only kill and it makes me angry to think that the only thing some people remember is that some twisted soldiers did kill innocent people and dump them in a mass grave. We had not lost our respect for human life because we had to fight in an unpopular war."

"To tell the truth, I have no regrets. I feel I spent more time helping rather than fighting. I want people to know that I wasn't alone in my efforts either. The helicopter pilots put their life on the line both for our men and the Vietnamese civilians without any hesitation. I did get a medal of valor from the Navy, and I'm proud of it."

Breaking the Silence

BOB AND CRICKET were two army soldiers who returned from Vietnam. Cricket was quiet but friendly, while Bob never spoke a word. Bob and Cricket had served in 'Nam and lost most of the men in their company.

According to Cricket and two other vets who were also with Bob, it was hell from the beginning. Relying on tunnel rats to keep track of the enemy and numerous ambushes, it seemed as if they were always under fire. Too little sleep and too many men being killed almost daily drove Bob into a deep depression to the point that he stopped talking to anyone.

Bob was an attractive man and there were several hostesses who tried talking to him, but he acted as if they weren't even there. He seldom made eye contact and showed no emotion. Eventually, they all left him alone, thinking he was Looney.

Bob was a very sensitive man who was having a hard time dealing with the futility of the war and reacted to it by trying to shut-out the world around him. Those of us who knew him would talk to him if only to acknowledge the fact that he was there and that we cared.

Bob was Cricket's shadow. Wherever Cricket went he'd follow or at the USO if Cricket was playing pool, Bob would sit in front of the TV. Often after the USO closed for the evening, when we would go out for a hamburger and fries, Cricket would just order the same thing for Bob. Cricket was a very patient and understanding friend to Bob.

When we were at the USO, Cricket and I liked to play a card game called spades. To play, you needed at least two couples to make it fun and Cricket and I were always partners. After sitting in on so many games, Bob knew how to play.

One day we needed another couple and we got another hostess named Dianne to be Bob's partner. Bob would hold up his fingers to indicate how many tricks he could win with his hand. We ended up playing several games and were happy to see that Bob enjoyed playing the game. We became a regular foursome after that.

Slowly, Bob began to change. He made more eye contact with us as we played cards. At pool, Bob would point to a pockets and smile when he made the shot. He began to laugh. His shell was starting to crack.

After several weeks of being a foursome, when it came time to count the tricks we could get with our hand, instead of using his fingers, Bob suddenly spoke and said four. Cricket, Dianne and I looked at each other to confirm what we had heard. Bob began saying hi and like a young child, his spoken vocabulary began to extend to full sentences.

Dianne was a very kind person and she and Bob brought out the best in each other. It became obvious that the two of them had developed a deep affection for each other and we were thrilled for them.

Bob could not have had a more understanding friend than Cricket, but I think it was the patience and love of Dianne that brought him back in touch with others and helped him leave his past nightmare behind.

The Returning Veterans

THE VIETNAM "CONFLICT" had officially ended. Hanoi was releasing 591 POW/MIAs and they were flying home. The airport where they were arriving was full of dignitaries, family and friends along with well wishers, waiting to welcome our servicemen home.

A group of us from the USO, both servicemen and hostesses, got together in the early morning to watch the unfolding story of the hundreds of service men arriving back from Vietnam. The event was broadcasted live across America. Many of us were wearing our POW/MIA bracelet, a metal band inscribed with the soldiers name and the date he was captured or reported missing.

We waited with anticipation for our soldier to emerge from one of the planes carrying the men. When anyone's soldier was announced, they took off their bracelet and put it on a table.

The broadcast was emotional as the haggard men appeared, often with a slight smile and tears. By the time the last serviceman was shown, the flag waving crowd was cheering, crying and clapping; drowning out the announcer. The soldiers received a well deserved welcome home.

I looked down at my wrist and the bracelet that I was still wearing. My soldier along with hundreds of others did not come home. For the families of those men, they had to continue to endure the heartache of not knowing their loved ones fate. There were too many servicemen about whom we would never know.

The war was over but the emotional wounds of many Vietnam Veterans would take a long time to heal. Many were struggling to get their lives back together and were having a difficult time adjusting to civilian life which was often plagued with nightmares and depression.

Unfortunately, dreams, depression and thoughts of suicide affected too many veterans; especially the men who saw the worst of the fighting. They were still haunted by the war and out country's lack of support. A Vietnam Veteran told me "you may be home, but the war never leaves you."

The Summer Camp

DUE TO LACK of funds, the Baltimore USO closed its doors. With time, the other hostesses and I eventually drifted apart. The Vietnam War was finally over. I quit ushering at the theatre. The only thing that remained constant was my job with my dad. I felt as if my world had totally changed and it meant starting over.

Sometimes the warm summer's sun fades and you change with it. My summer became autumn, changing into a cold, lonely winter. I chose to become a loner for a time, maybe too long. Maybe it was losing so many people in my life that made me cold and kept me distant from other people.

But, I will always regret that the person who had once been nicknamed "sunshine" was gone. Somehow, that part of me died. I felt lost in a crowd, with no sense of direction and no desire to become involved.

A long time friend knew I was going through a hard time and called to see if I would consider at helping out a summer camp for children stricken with cerebral palsy. Pam taught children with Cerebral Palsy and I had gone to her classroom a few times to help her with special events. Years ago, Pam had given me a book by Christi Brown called *My Left Foot* and I had been touched by it.

The summer camp needed volunteers, so I made arrangements with my dad to take the time off. It would not only give me a chance to help someone else, but also help myself by becoming involved with something besides myself.

Thinking I was familiar enough with what to expect, I was confident enough to think it wouldn't bother me to work with these children. After all, I told myself, I had been around handicapped children before.

Boy was I wrong! For the first three days, I would come home and cry all evening. All day, I'd fight to hold back the tears. I didn't think I could work at the camp and was ready to quit. When I talked to Pam about it, she admitted that she too had felt that way many times. I decided that since I committed myself for the two weeks, I would follow it through.

Before, I had been around children who were retarded and often didn't realize how bad off they really were. But now, I had been assigned to a little black boy named Steve who was as smart as a whip.

Steve was severely crippled and had pressure sores over his entire body from sitting too long in his wheelchair. His arms and legs were twisted in an awkward position, making it difficult for him to even sit up.

Steve had to be strapped into his chair. My heart ached for him! "Oh God, why?" I'd ask and yet I'd look at him and see a happy child with sparkling eyes.

"Come on Karen, let's win the race!" he shouted one day. That day, we were having a big race. Each volunteer would push their child in their wheelchair on a special course. If I ever wanted to win a race, it was then.

It wasn't easy but we won the race. I don't remember what Steve won, but my prize was seeing the smile on that happy little boy's face.

During those two weeks, I had learned a lot about commitment, acceptance, giving and love. There were a lot of dedicated people who gave it their all, not only for two weeks out of the summer, but year round.

I met a lot of people I really admired, especially Steve, the little boy who opened my heart and eyes and let the sun shine in.

Chapter Two

Great Adventures

Bratislava

Paris

Across a Crowded Room

Dinner on The Seine

The Voice

A Week to Remember

La Vie en Rose

Letters and Phone Calls

New French Stories

Christmas in Paris

On the Street Where we Live

The Tailor and the Seamstress

The Magic Telephone

Robert and the Decision

The Lebanese Embassy

Bon Voyage

Bratislava

O N A TRIP to Vienna, we were taking a cruise to Bratislava, Czechoslovakia, off the banks of the Danube River. During the cruise, we had a tour guide who pointed out landmarks or different points of interest. As she was talking, I sat close to the edge of the boat letting the spray of the water hit my face.

The weather was both chilly and cloudy and the threat of rain stayed with us most of the day. Since hearing about the trip down the romantic blue Danube, I had been looking forward to it. To my disappointment, the Danube was an ugly, murky green color, a far cry from being romantic and blue.

The Danube River is a lot lower than Bratislava and as we got closer, we could see a bridge going across the Danube, lined with people. Our guide told us that the people liked to see Americans in their bright colored clothes.

They watched us as we got off the boat and up the ramp to their city. All the people were fenced in and could not get out. Our guide said she would not be joining us and introduced us to the man who would accompany us on our tour of Bratislava.

As we were getting ready to depart from the boat, I made a quick trip to the ladies room. As I washed my hands, I noticed our tour guide standing at the window watching the people lined up around the fence.

As I got closer to her to throw away the paper towel I used, I heard her softly crying. I asked her if she was OK. She slowly turned towards me. With tears streaming down her face, she told me part of her story.

Years ago, she had escaped Czechoslovakia and gone to Austria where she lived. Because of that, she had to stay on the boat. She told me that the people lined up every day a foreign ship came to its port, hoping to find a way of escaping.

Some people, in desperation, would jump off the bridge across the Danube and if they survived the fall into the water, they tried to swim to freedom. I felt bad for her and told her I was sorry, it must be hard for her. She gave me a faint smile and told me to hurry up before everyone left without me.

The streets of Bratislava looked empty, a sharp contrast to the bustling, beautiful city of Vienna. My first impression of the city was that I was walking through an old black and white movie. Time seemed to have stood still and everything looked gray.

Slowly approaching our direction, was a young soldier looking proud in his uniform and his girl looking at him as only a young girl in love would look at her man, with her arm wrapped through his.

Before starting our tour of the city, we were to have lunch. As we were served warm Coke in a bottle, the waiters took the caps off the bottles and quickly grabbed them as if they were precious. I thought it was just my reaction to the way they grabbed the caps but I heard someone else say, "We weren't going to keep them anyway."

We were served soup, with a clear broth and two meatballs with very few noodles. It was good but I was more interested in watching the people who served us food and how they watched us, than in eating.

As we walked along the streets and past the old buildings, I couldn't help but notice that this city definitely had a charm of its own. Some of the sights had included the medieval town hall, the cathedral and ruins of the palace of Schlossberg. Kings of Hungary were once crowned in Bratislava long ago.

The day had gone quickly and it was time to head back to the boat and back to Vienna. As I watched the people of Bratislava, I thought about how pitiful it was to think that some people agreed with the idea that people should have to be fenced in their own country like criminals. People, like butterflies, should be able to put on their most colorful outfit and fly wherever they wanted to go.

The tour guide, once again composed, was waiting for us as we boarded. We smiled at one another. Inside that seemingly proper and snobbish exterior of hers', there was a very soft person. Alone, I sat close to the edge of the boat and looked down at the Danube. It didn't seem as murky and ugly as it had before. As the setting sun broke through the clouds, the Danube began to sparkle and dance, to a tune of its own.

Paris

ONE DAY, AS I was sorting through our mail at work, I came across a brochure from the Maryland State Dental Association. The dentists were planning a trip to Paris in the spring. Paris! Oh, how I've always wanted to go there. I waited for my dad to finish with his patient to show him the brochure.

"Wouldn't you just love to go to Paris, Dad?" I asked. My excitement was obvious but he just smiled. After discussing the trip, my parents decided to go and as long as I paid my own way, I could go too.

Saving up for the trip and keeping up with my rent and other bills left me with very little money left over. But, I managed to buy some patterns and material to make a few outfits for the trip. Paris, the fashion capital of the world, was one place where I wanted to be well dressed.

Before we knew it, the big day had arrived and we boarded the plane to Paris. Once the plane was airborne, many of us got up from our seats and began to mingle with the others.

On the plane I saw two couples I had gotten to know in Vienna and after talking with them for a while, they asked me why I wasn't married yet. I just shrugged and smiled at them. I had turned 25 in February and I didn't feel old enough to worry about being single forever.

Not yet anyway. One of the dentists winked at me as he said to be careful. He had heard about a certain magic in Paris during the spring. We all laughed. It was a good group to be going with and I was very excited.

After landing and going through customs, we were all ushered to a bus that took us to our hotel. Our tour guide pointed out different sites along the way. He reminded us to change our watches and told us we should have plenty of time to unpack and take a nap or relax before we all met again later for our cruise and dinner on the Seine that evening.

Once I got to the hotel room and unpacked, I tried to sleep but was too keyed up. Since it was my first night in Paris, I didn't want to waste a minute of it. I took a shower and started to get dressed for the evening a little early.

Except for the final touch of perfume, I was ready for my dinner cruise and grabbed my crocheted shawl in case it got chilly. Having plenty of time to spare, I decided to go to the hotel lounge for a glass of wine and then go to the lobby to wait for the dental group to gather.

Across a Crowded Room

THE LOUNGE HAD been quiet compared to the busy lobby. People were everywhere. Every seat was taken and people lined the walls. Across the crowded room, he caught my eye. I thought he was one of the most handsome men I had ever seen.

He was talking to a friend when he looked up and noticed me looking at him. Embarrassed, I took a cigarette out of my purse and fumbled for my matches. He walked over to me and offered me a light. He said nothing but smiled as I said thank you.

"Oh you speak English," his friend said. His friend then introduced himself, his name was Pierre and his friend was Omar.

They both looked about my age. Omar's brown eyes and jet black hair enhanced his olive complexion while Pierre was fair in comparison with his light brown hair. Omar spoke French and Pierre spoke English.

Both of them were students in Paris. They had come to the hotel to meet a friend who was flying into Paris and would meet them in the lobby when he arrived.

After I mentioned I had just arrived and was anxious to see the sights they offered to show me around Paris the next day and I accepted their offer. We talked until I noticed some of our group beginning to gather. We said goodbye and agreed to meet the next morning.

Dinner on the Seine

I T WAS A warm, clear evening. The air had a lovely fragrance of blossoms and as with spring, everything looked fresh and new. I couldn't have asked for a better evening to take a cruise.

The boat we were boarding was a long barge that had been converted into a restaurant. The tables were elegantly dressed with linens, flowers and candles. My parents and I sat down at a table close to the edge of the boat and when everyone had been seated, our cruise began.

The sun was beginning to set, leaving beautiful pink, blue and lavender colors in the sky that reflected on the water. The small white lights that outlined the boat flickered on the water.

On the upper deck, couples were dancing to the music that drifted down to our tables as we floated past the Eiffel Tower, the Louvre and Note Dame Cathedral. It was all so beautiful and romantic.

I thought of Omar as I watched the different couples who strolled along the pathway at the edge of the flowing river walking arm in arm or holding hands. My parents left their table to visit with another couple they knew, leaving me alone to day dream as I gazed upon the lovely river Seine; it was going to be an exciting week.

The Voice

O MAR, PIERRE AND I met the next morning and set out to see some of the sites of Paris. While we were walking around, Pierre reminded Omar that they were to meet with some friends at Pierre's apartment. Since we were close by, I was invited to join them.

When we arrived at Pierre's, several of their friends and his roommate were already there. Not long after I was introduced to everyone, three more men arrived. They were greeted warmly with hugs and kisses on both cheeks, a traditional greeting. They had brought food and messages from home.

We all sat on the floor in a large circle. Bread, olives, cheese, pastries, pistachios and a special meat called Bastirma (which brought cheers) were put on plates and in bowls and placed in front of us.

Someone had brought some fresh fruit and cheese from a local market. Those who had brought or received something special from home shared their treasures with everyone. All of us were offered a cup of Arabic coffee and then began to eat as some of the men began talking to one another.

The conversation seemed to go from pleasant to more intense. Pierre told me everyone was speaking Arabic. Not knowing much about Omar and Pierre, I had assumed they were Arabs if they spoke Arabic.

Several guys were getting very loud and angry, while the others became very quiet and listened to the conversation, occasionally joining in. I began to feel very out of place and wondered if I had made a smart decision by going there.

I was scared and wanted to step back for a few minutes, so I excused myself and went into the bathroom.

"Oh God, what am I doing here? These men could be your enemies," I said aloud but in a whisper.

A voice, very clear, not my own or one that I had heard before said, firmly but gently, "Anyone who loves me is not my enemy!"

I got chills all over my body. I had just heard a voice that had been very real. I looked around the bathroom. I wondered if he could have been God's voice. Confused and a little shaken, I left the bathroom to join everyone else.

When I came back, the tension seemed to have eased up and I sat down next to Omar. The St. Christopher medal that I wore (usually under my clothes) was in clear view. Omar gently took it in his hands and asked if I were a Christian, in Lebanese.

Pierre translated what Omar had asked into English. I said "yes, I am a Christian." Omar smiled and said that they were all Christians too. As I looked closely at the circle of men, I noticed that most of them had either a cross or religious medal around their necks.

One of them spoke English very well and told me that they were all Christians from Beirut, Lebanon. He told me about the war between the Christians and Muslims and explained why everyone had gotten so upset.

The French government granted permanent visas to anyone from Lebanon, so many Lebanese men came to Paris for work and would send the money home to their families.

They began to talk about their faith in God and how important it was to them to be a Christian. In Beirut, people were being killed because of their religion and I admired them for their commitment to their beliefs.

I thought it was both sad and ironic that religion separated people and divided nations rather than bringing everyone together.

God did not make religions; he gave us rules to live by. I felt very sad after hearing about the war. I was offered and accepted a cup of hot tea. Everyone seemed relieved to have the war update over with and out of the way.

As I nursed my cup of tea, I thought about the voice and wondered why I had heard it. I had to leave and meet the dental group, so I had to say goodbye. Many of the men I met that day I would meet again on my pilgrimage that awaited me on my path in life.

A Week to Remember

PARIS WAS A fabulous city combining the old and the new. The city had a unique charm. One week was not enough time to see all the sights. If the tour guide had nothing planned, our group had the opportunity to do and see what we wanted.

The remaining days of the week had been full of activities; a tour of the wine country in Loire Valley, a trip to the Palace of Versailles and lunch at Momarte.

On my last full day in Paris, Omar and I spent the day walking around Paris. I had wanted to see Jim Morrison's grave, but it was not on the dental group's itinerary, so I asked Omar if he would take me there and he did. After that we went to Notre Dame Cathedral and then walked along the Seine, on the brick pavement, until we came to the Eiffel Tower.

We asked another tourist to take a picture of us in front of the fountain with the Eiffel Tower as the backdrop. As we were running hand in hand around the fountain and the famous tower, I became aware of the fact that it wasn't the running that made my heart flutter, but Omar.

To help us communicate, my French/English, English/French dictionary served as our interpreter. Walking up and down the Paris streets, we stopped at a café where we drank several cups of tea and coffee while eating a French pastry.

Omar had complimented me on my clothes and he mentioned that he was taking classes in clothes designing. We went to the apartment he shared with his brother, Robert, to see the sketches Omar had designed for his homework.

They were beautiful gowns and dresses. As an accomplished seamstress in my own right, I could appreciate his talent in creating a design and the pattern to make the garment.

Omar told me about this tailor shop in Beirut where he would make a made to order suit, but he wanted to expand his business by including designer clothes for women. Because of the war, business in Beirut was in a decline.

We talked about our faith being an important part of our lives, and although our cultures were worlds apart, I felt that the strongest bond two people could share, mentally, was that of a common faith, and in our case, Christianity.

Before I left Paris for home, I gave Omar the Saint Christopher medal I wore, which was inscribed with the words, "You'll never walk alone." I had a very strong feeling I would be leaving a special person behind. As I gave Omar the necklace, I promised Omar I would come back to Paris.

La Vie en Rose

O N OUR LAST night in Paris, the dental group went out to dinner to one of our tour guides favorite restaurants. The restaurant was located on the West Bank, close to Notre Dame. From the street, we walked down three steps into the front door. The restaurant was very long with a large bay window in the front. Because of the size of our group, the tables were moved to form two long tables on each side of the restaurant.

In front by the window was a small area for a group to play, which, that night, consisted of two accordion players and a violinist. All three of the men were wearing the traditional black beret and red scarf. One of the accordion players was the man who was the speaker and singer for the group.

After playing a few songs, he asked if anyone had any requests and I, along with several others, raised our hands. My request was La Vie en Rose, a French love song. The group walked around the large room as they played and sang, walking close to the person who requested the song they were playing.

The singer had a beautiful voice and the song was well played. By the time they had finished the song I had tears in my eyes. Hearing that song and being in Paris was something I had dreamed of. I thanked the three of them, and the singer kissed my hand.

The carafes of wine on the tables were continually being refilled with wine and by the end of the meal; we had a very lively group when we left the restaurant.

After we were all on the bus, our driver drove around the many landmarks in Paris. Although Paris is a beautiful city during the day, Paris, the city of lights, is lovely and romantic at night when it is lit up.

The evening was a perfect ending to our vacation. Being the romantic that I am, La Vie en Rose always brings back memories of my trip to Paris. It was sad to leave Paris; the city was everything I had ever dreamed it would be. In leaving, I was leaving a bit of my heart to both the city and Omar.

On the long flight home, I felt emptiness and knew that there was something special about my relationship with Omar. In time, it would be clear to me what it was.

I knew part of what I was feeling was the excitement of Paris and meeting a handsome man. The voice I had heard in the bathroom was still very clear in my mind, and it was something that I would not take lightly.

Letters and Phone Calls

AFTER MY TRIP to Paris, life quickly went back to my normal routine. I spent a lot of time daydreaming about what it would be like to live and work in Paris with Omar. Before leaving Paris, Omar and I exchanged addresses and he had my phone number, so I looked forward to hearing from him.

I was so excited when I received my first letter from him but it was written in French. Fortunately, one of my sisters-in-law was fluent in French and translated the letter. Knowing Omar has friends who spoke English, I wrote to him in English.

Sometimes I would receive letters in English but in a different handwriting. Occasionally he would call me and we would talk, mixing English and French in our conversations.

For several months we wrote back and forth at least once a week, and I began writing more letters in French, although they would take me a lot longer, and I needed to consult my French/English dictionary.

Omar would write about his feelings asking me if and when I was coming back to Paris. He assured me he could find me a job. In return I told him that I hoped to come back but that I needed to save some money first. The thought of going back to Paris and living there was a romantic one, and I spent hours thinking about it.

The news on TV began to have nightly segments on civil war in Lebanon. I often thought how difficult it must be for Omar and his friends to heat about what was going on in their country.

Because so many Lebanese would go back and forth from Paris to Beirut, those who remained in Paris were given an accurate account of what was going on as well as checking on their families and friends.

In Omar's letters he would sometimes write about Beirut, but as we continued to write, he wrote more about his hopes and dreams of the future. The letters revealed more of him and I began to feel closer to him and wanted to be part of his life.

I began talking to my parents about Omar, my feelings, and my desire to go back to Paris and work there. I didn't need their permission but I did want their approval. They realized that going was something I was serious about and reluctantly they gave me their approval.

I was happier than I had been in the last few years since my time at the USO, and I felt I should follow my dream of living in Paris.

I knew that I would have to have enough money to live over there until I did get a job. I still had to buy a round trip ticket in case it didn't work out. I got a part time job in the evenings that did not conflict with my day job.

After a few months of working I sold my car and bought a round trip "open ticket" to Paris that was good for one year. I wrote to Omar telling him about selling my car and buying my ticket and he was pleased I was coming over.

We had planned on my coming over in November. I was both nervous and excited at the same time. I thought about the voice and believed it was my destiny to go back to Paris and Omar.

Dave encouraged me to follow my dream and give it a chance. Dave was the only person I had told about hearing the voice.

We wrote until it was time to go and Omar called to make sure he knew the correct flight number and day and time of my arrival. I didn't have much to do to prepare for Paris except to decide what clothes or anything else I might want or need.

New French Stories

I T WAS THANKSGIVING Day and since my parents were driving me to the airport for my flight to Paris, we went to a restaurant for a proper Thanksgiving dinner. My brothers were scattered around the country that year and a flight to Paris was cheaper if I flew on the holiday.

Except for the time Bruce was in Vietnam, it was the first Thanksgiving my parents, brothers, and I weren't together. But it was still a special day, considering the situation.

After dinner it was time to head for the airport and before long, it was time for passengers to board the plane. After hugs, kisses and the "I love you" between us, my dad said, "this will either be the best decision or the worst mistake you ever make."

I was about to start another adventure in my life. If I hadn't felt so strongly about Omar, I would not have been flying to Paris. Paris would be a new adventure. I had dreamed of living in the romantic, "City of Lights."

As I boarded the plane after my last wave goodbye, I was scared, excited, crying, and missing my family and home already. As the stewardess came around offering the passengers a drink, I had a hot tea and tried to relax. It would be a long flight.

The airport was huge. The Charles de Gaulle airport was a "hub" for planes to refuel or for passengers to catch connecting flights to their destination as well as flights to France. After finding my luggage and going through customs, I saw Omar at the gate holding flowers and my heart skipped a beat. I was as excited as I was nervous but it was too late to turn back now.

After going through Customs and gathering my luggage, I went through the doors and into the waiting area. Omar was there to greet me with flowers. My heart skipped a beat when I saw him.

After a hug and a kiss, Omar helped me gather up my luggage. Omar hailed a cab to the hotel where we had a room.

The hotel where we would be staying was in the Latin Quarters by the West Bank off St Michelle. Many of the hotel patrons were students who rented the room by the week or the month. The rooms were affordable for most students.

The room was large with high ceilings and long French windows and a sink. The showers and bathrooms were down the hall. The hotel was old but well kept and clean.

On the Street Where We Live

OMAR WAS STUDYING dress designing and had made arrangements with his teacher to take some time off school as long as he kept ups with his homework. We needed some time to get situated and for me to learn my way around Paris.

Our hotel was just off the Boulevard St Michelle and a block to the left was the Boulevard St Germaine. The area we lived in was known as the Latin Quarters. While the area around Champs Elysee and the Place de la Concorde was full of designer shops, posh restaurants and cafes where the more affluent Parisians frequented. The Latin Quarter was lower key, but it has had a charm of its own with seemingly endless shops, cafes and restaurants.

The streets were full of merchants, artists, students and tourists. There were a lot of well known sights and elaborate buildings close by. Walking down the street we stopped in a bakery for a cup of tea and a pastry as we watched the Fountain St. Michelle with its small courtyard full of people. Further down the street along the boulevard, artists sat and sketched scenery, and street vendors lined the wall by the Seine, selling their artwork.

Across the Seine was the beautiful Cathedral of Notre Dame and across from that was the fabulous Louvre. Standing in front of Notre Dame, the Eiffel Tower could be seen along the Seine. A statue an exact replica of the

Statue of Liberty was also in view. The section across the Seine with Notre Dame and the Louvre was known as the West Bank.

We went on the Metro and headed over the Montmartre where we visited some of Omar's friends. We had lunch on the courtyard surrounding Montmartre and watched the artists at work. As the day turned to evening, we went to the beautiful Sacre Coeur and sat on the steps overlooking the city. It had been a long day and we headed back to the hotel.

I could not believe how fortunate I was to be on the street where we lived.

The Tailor and the Seamstress

Omar was studying dress designing. He was a tailor but hoped to begin designing and sewing women's clothes. Omar's sketched were beautiful evening dresses and gowns; elegant and stylish. Unfortunately, money was a problem. The money I had brought with me was gone and the small amount Omar received for school went to pay for the hotel room.

Omar was a student and going to classes, so the school provided meal tickets for the school's canteen. The canteen provided a complete meal with a beverage and dessert. Fruit, yogurt and a small container of mile was also available which we usually took back to our room for breakfast.

By my using a ticket, it was half the tickets Omar was used to. Omar realized he would have to quit school and find a job. Both of us needed to work to afford to continue to live in the Latin Quarters.

We found work at a small factory above a dress shop. The store was in an area of Paris where buyers would come for clothes to distribute to different stores. We worked together for several weeks for a woman from Spain.

She spoke only Spanish and French so we spoke very little to one another. But fortunately, we sewed piecework and she would show me a finished collar or sleeve and cuff and I would know what she wanted.

For a while, I thought it was great a great job and I liked working there. I wondered who would end up wearing the dress I was sewing. Weeks later, a man looking for work came in the shop and our boss gave him my job.

He was faster than I was and in the garment making business, speed is as important as accuracy. In her own way, I knew she felt awkward about letting me go, but it was her livelihood and a very competitive business. Time was money.

We parted on good terms. Omar continued to work, but we barely get by. Without the help of a few friends, we never would have made it.

Christmas in Paris

THE FRAGRANT SMELL of chestnuts roasting over the vendor's coals mingled through the crowd. Crêpes, with their sweet aroma, was being cooked on the corners of the busy Paris streets. Christmas carols in French and English, being played in different stores, could be heard as we walked down the street. Last-minute shoppers crowded the sidewalks carrying packages as they hurried to finish their Christmas shopping before the stores closed.

The city of lights was even brighter than usual. The stores and trees along the sidewalks were lit with delicate, white lights. Candles on the tables of the glass enclosed cafés, twinkled on the window panes. A fine snow fell from the sky making Christmas Eve. seem like a winter wonderland.

Omar and I made our way through the busy streets to Notre Dame Cathedral to hear the choir sing. Slipping into one of the back pews, we sat back and relaxed as the choir sang. The church was both warm and full. Many of the carols the choir sang were familiar to me and they sounded beautiful being sung in French.

After church, we both bought a crêpe with sugar and butter, a luxury for someone with little money. We walked down the steps that led us to the banks of the Seine and sat on the bench as we ate our crepes. The lights from the buildings and streets above the Seine reflected on the dark, cold water.

Even though I was happy being with Omar, something was missing from Christmas. I missed my family and the States. Being with Omar did not replace Christmas traditions. After eating our crepes, we went back to the hotel.

We were joining friends for Christmas dinner and all of us Omar, Roman, George and I were missing our homes. Roman did his best to make the day as festive as possible by making a few traditional Lebanese favorites.

Roman and I talked about our different family traditions as I helped him make some of the dishes. Omar became moody, depressed and frustrated at not having money and being far away from home. When George reminded him that we were all away from home, Omar became angry. I told Omar to cheer up. With that, Omar became even angrier and slapped me across my face. His hand hit my eye, causing it to tear and turn red. Roman jumped up from his chair, grabbing Omar in my defense.

Omar was told to control his temper which made him angrier causing him to leave the apartment. I thought of taking my return ticket to the states and flying home. But my pride stopped me.

I worked hard to get to Paris but I was miserable. I defended Omar's actions though, knowing he had been worried about his family because of the war in Beirut. Several hours after Omar left he returned.

Omar apologized and said he would never lose his temper or hit me again. I accepted his apology. Even though our relationship had gotten off to a bad start, I was determined to make it work. I still carry a scar of that day as a red streak across my right eye.

The Magic Telephone

JUST WHEN I got to the point when I really needed a bit of home I'd see a line of people beside a telephone booth anxiously awaiting their turn. It only meant one thing, the magic phone, as I called it, was working. With the magic telephone you could talk to anyone, anywhere in the world, for free.

There was a certain way to fiddle with the receiver tab to open the line and then insert a piece of neatly folded paper just so, or you could lose the line. There were times when two or three people would use the phone only to lose the line and we couldn't get it back, leaving many people disappointed. It wasn't always easy or possible to get an open line. With a three-year waiting period for private phone line in Paris, we knew very few people with a phone.

The French police were becoming aware of what was going on, so they knew to watch for telephones with a crowd gathered around it, or one with a long line. So, if there were a lot of people waiting to use the telephone, we would separate into small groups depending on what language you spoke.

We walked far enough away from the phone to not be obvious but close enough to watch for our turn. You could say the phone brought some people together for a time and I met some interesting people while I was waiting for my turn. Luckily for me, the night was the best time for me to call home in my part of the world and police didn't bother with the phones at night.

The first time I used the phone was shortly after arriving in Paris. Sal, a friend of Roman, Omar and George, told us about a phone in the courtyard behind our apartment. I had never heard about it before and was a little skeptical. But Omar told me that was how he called me in the States. Omar grabbed my hand to help me up from the chair I was sitting in.

Grabbing our coats we hurried down the stairs and outside with Roman, George and Sal in the lead. Another friend of Sal's was on the line. They had managed to get a line through to Beirut which wasn't easy to do because so many times the lines were down because of the fighting. When Omar was on the phone, he was talking to his parents about me and then handed me the phone. All I could say in Lebanese was "hello", "how are you," "I am fine," and "goodbye". So went my first introduction and communication with Omar's parents.

I knew what we were doing was wrong, and at first I refused to use the phone to call home. Since tapping the phone is illegal I was worried about whether or not they could trace the call to my parents or that I'd get caught.

The last thing I wanted was trouble with the French government. But everyone else had talked to their families so I took a chance. Roman dialed my number for me and told me that if at any time I saw a policeman I should take out the paper and hang up. Luckily, no one came by, and my parents were thrilled to hear from me.

One cold and rainy Saturday afternoon, there was a fairly large crowd of foreigners in our courtyard. The government started fixing some of the more popular phones so they couldn't be toyed with, but Roman managed to get an open line since no one had fixed this one.

With eight benches full of people and a few people pacing up and down the pavement, we would have attracted attention but this was like having our own sanctuary, just outside Paris city limits.

Everyone in the courtyard was friendly and embraced that kind of comradery with fellow travelers. If a phone line stays open and working long enough, word spreads like a brush fire. Some people would wait their turn to use the phone and leave while others stayed to talk with different people in the group.

As travelers waited patiently for their turn, they would exchange travel tips, and addresses of inexpensive places to eat and sleep, or talk about where they had been or where they were going.

Among the people gathered, there was a Canadian couple visiting London and Paris, backpacking and saving no more money than if they had stayed at cheap hotels. There was a Swedish man also traveling through France before heading home.

Omar was talking to a group of Lebanese about the current situation in Beirut. Roman was flirting with two young ladies from England and the only other American besides me was having a last fling with freedom before he went back to the States to enter law school.

Most of the people just called home to say hello and that they were OK. Only one guy said he called home to ask for money. Omar and I had the bombshells; since we were going to Beirut, we had to tell our parents what was going on.

Omar's parents were thrilled while mine were very concerned and upset with my decision. I was feeling scared and low in spirit myself after talking to them. My parents wanted me to come home.

The rain had become heavier. Those of us, who remained, decided to continue our conversations in the café next door. Someone who chose to remain anonymous treated us to our choice of tea, coffee or hot chocolate. The conversations continued through most of the evening.

Because of the magic telephone, there were many times I had gotten to talk to my parents when without it, talking to them would have been impossible. Not all my phone calls were made illegally. But, right or wrong, the magic phone gave us a chance to touch base with some of the people who were so important to us.

Robert and the Decision

AFTER ALMOST THREE months of living in Paris, my visa was running out of time. To renew it, I had to prove I could support myself in Paris or leave France. Not having a job or our own place to live was a big problem. Paris was an expensive city to live in. Wages in the dress shop barely covered the cost of our room with very little left over for food.

If I left France for a day or two, I could go to England and get another visa for three more months. I was familiar enough with London to know my way around to get to the U.S. Embassy. But going to England and waiting on a visa for France would have cost more money than we had. My only choices were to go home or go to Lebanon with Omar.

Knowing our dilemma, Omar's brother Robert had offered to pay for our tickets if we decided to go to Lebanon. Beirut was not the best place to be at that time. What if war broke out again while we were there and we couldn't leave? A man at the American embassy did not think it was the wisest decision to go to Beirut. But the American embassy would be open and if something did happen, I could take refuge there.

Omar wanted me to go with him to Beirut and meet his family. Omar also wanted me to meet Omar's family and for them to meet me. Omar's mother was sick with cancer and wanted to see him. Besides, I told myself, I should meet Omar's family and know more about him before we got married.

One evening, Omar and I were standing on the platform waiting for the next Metro. The Metro station was empty, giving us privacy to talk. Talking about his family and how we both missed home, made me feel lonely.

Omar looked down and nervously shuffled his feet. He looked so sad. It was obvious Omar longed to see his family. It had been over a year since he had been to Beirut.

"Robert told me my mom is dying of cancer," he said.
"I don't want her to die before we see each other again."

The idea of going to Beirut worried me because of the civil unrest, but at the same time, going to Lebanon excited me. Going to Lebanon was not an easy decision to make, but I loved Omar and wanted to see him happy. I turned to Omar and told him that I would go with him. A smile appeared on his face, and he hugged me as the Metro pulled into the station. On the way back to the motel, we went over to Robert's apartment. He seemed pleased to know that we were taking him up on his offer.

For Omar and I to be married in Paris we had to have been there for a full three months and have had all medical forms and tests completed. Once again, it was lack of money that got in our way. So before we left Robert that night, he gave us the money to go to a doctor to complete all the medical tests.

If we timed that trip to Lebanon properly, we could come back to Paris, the medical papers would have been completed, and we could file for our marriage license. With the money for a visa and tickets, we had to get busy with the medical tests and get my visa for Lebanon as soon as possible before my visa for Paris ran out.

Before we left Robert's apartment, he told me he wanted to take me shopping the next day. I was to meet Robert in the morning, and he would also take me to lunch. We would meet Omar when we were finished and when his work day was over.

Robert was the second oldest of six children. He was two years younger than Samir the eldest son and three years older than Omar. Robert and I were the same age. Robert was a good looking man but very serious.

He carried a lot of weight on his shoulders, worrying about his parents and siblings in Beirut. His father had a small grocery store, but food and other supplies did not always get to him due to the fighting. So, Robert sent them money to take care of them.

Robert had come to Paris several years before I met him to study dress design. He was very talented and creative and his styles were popular. Many of them were made into clothes. Robert worked very hard and got along very well with people. He spent long hours traveling.

Robert had a job as a buyer. Eventually, he had stores in Beirut, New York, San Francisco and Florida. He sold the store in Beirut and opened one in Palm Springs. Robert worked in Paris both as a designer and buyer, but did not own a store there.

In Lebanon, it was not proper attire for a woman to wear pants, especially jeans, so he bought me several dresses, all very lovely. As a special gift, he took me shopping for a wedding gown and the one we did choose was beautiful. I was excited and didn't feel like a simple thank you was enough, but he was pleased I was marrying Omar and felt that I was a good influence on him.

I knew that Omar and I had put a strain on Robert because he was aware of the fact that we were barely getting by. Robert had always done what he could to help us out. It often seemed like he was giving Omar money.

He had us for dinner often. He was upset with Omar because Robert felt he wasn't doing the best he could to find a better job. When Omar did have money he wasn't as wise with it as he should have been.

To help save money, I washed our clothes in the sink, hung them to dry and made meals with the Bunsen burner. Robert was aware that Omar did not want me to work, but did not say anything about it.

Looking back, I think it was more a matter of control Omar had on me rather than the pride of being the provider. But, at the time, I didn't see it.

The Lebanese Embassy

AFTER WE HAD completed the medical tests, we got on the Metro to go to the Victor Hugo Station to the Lebanese Embassy. The Embassy seemed so small compared to the U.S. Embassy. The iron gate around the embassy opened to the small courtyard outside the building.

The men who worked in the embassy were both friendly and helpful. After greeting us warmly, we handed a man the passports and he began speaking to me in English.

"You want to go to Beirut?" He asked.

"Yes, my fiancé wants me to meet his family and show me Beirut," I said.

"Not much to see now," he replied."Do you speak Lebanese?"

"Very little," I said."But I am learning. I am more worried about the war. It is still quiet over there?" I continued.

"For now, but not many people are going to Lebanon now." His answer made me wonder if I was making a wise decision by going there.

"You should be safe going to Beirut. The fighting has stopped and many of the civilians who left because of the war are going home again," he reassured me.

Omar began to talk to the man and I walked around the room, looking at different pictures of Lebanon and studying a big map of the country. The paperwork was finished quickly. As I was handed my visa, the man wished us safe trip.

Down the street from the Embassy was a bakery. Fresh pastries had just been put on trays in the display shelves in the window. As someone was leaving the bakery, the aroma of fresh bread drifted through the opened door and onto the street. Without saying a word, Omar and I looked at each other and nodded in agreement. We went in and got a fresh pastry for each of us. Wanting to eat it warm, we sat on a bench by the bakery. As I ate my pastry, I thought about our trip to Lebanon.

I was already homesick, and here I was going to a country even further away with a different culture and affected by war. I had inherited my dad's "travel bug".

I enjoyed visiting new places and experience different cultures, but more than that was strong feeling that I was supposed to go there, to see Beirut, and meet his family. Little did I know then how important it was that I go.

Bon Voyage

TWO DAYS AFTER I got my visa to Lebanon, we were to leave Paris. Omar called the airlines to check if the baggage was within the limit. My baggage was too heavy, so something had to go. Before I came to Paris, I packed a few albums with me, the Moody Blues, the Eagles, and John Denver. I played them whenever a record player was available to me. So, I didn't want to part with them since the records were a bit of home for me.

I had several pairs of jeans which I had worn most of the time in Paris, but I would not be wearing them in Beirut, so I decided some of my jeans had to go. I put them in an old suitcase and left the suitcase in a busy park, hoping someone would open it and the jeans would be used by someone rather than being thrown away.

We didn't wait around to find out what became of them. Instead, we walked to one of our favorite places and got crêpes and tea. In less than 48 hours we would be in Lebanon.

After packing and paying for our room, our remaining time in Paris was our own. Since it was our last night in Paris before leaving for Beirut, we had decided to have a night on the town.

We had enough money to go to a nice restaurant for dinner, so on this rare occasion; we went to the Champs Elysee for dinner and strolled along the bustling boulevard. We ran into some friends as we were walking and they invited us to join them for coffee and tea.

The men spoke Lebanese and I had heard them mention Beirut several times while talking so I was glad that I did not understand most of what they were saying. I could tell that Omar was relaxed and enjoying himself.

Omar was anxious, excited, nervous, but happy to be going home. After saying goodbye and wishing us a bon voyage, we headed to Notre Dame.

The night sky was clear and filled with stars. The moon lit the path as we walked quietly along the Seine. A slight breeze drifted across the water causing the water to lightly spray our faces. Paris was so peaceful even with the traffic and people moving about.

Never in my wildest dreams did I ever imagine that I would be in Paris going to Beirut. Although I tried to think of going to Lebanon as an adventure, I was afraid to think about the war.

I had seen and heard how war can affect a person. I wondered how the people of Lebanon were coping with the war. Fighting was supposed to have stopped, but how long would that last?

Not wanting to ruin the lovely evening, I tried not to think about Beirut. We were tired after a long day of walking around the streets of Paris and went back to the hotel to get some sleep.

I was nervous the day we left. So much was uncertain, how long would we be there? How had the war affected the country? What would the people and culture be like? The threat of war was a big concern. We bought a tea and an espresso with our pastry as we headed for the Metro to the airport.

Boarding the plane, I hoped and prayed that things would be okay. I did my best not to worry about Beirut during our flight; it was too late to change my mind anyway.

Chapter 3

Lebanon, a Country at War

Beirut

A S WE EXITED the plane in Beirut, Syrian soldiers greeted us with rifles in hand. Omar's brother, Maroon, was at the airport to pick us up. Although he welcomed us warmly, he seemed tense and was anxious for us to get our luggage and go.

Beirut is a diverse city nestled between beautiful mountain ranges where sometimes the rocks jetted out to meet the coastline and a beach where the palm trees lined the outskirts of the beach.

Lebanon is a beautiful country and Beirut was called the Pearl of the Middle East. Before the war, Beirut was well known for its many universities as well as the beautiful beaches, the nightlife, the shopping districts and many cafes, giving it the air of Paris.

Even though I had watched the news about Lebanon on television and had heard stories from Omar and his friends, nothing had prepared me for what I saw in Beirut. Syrian soldiers in trucks and tanks patrol the streets. Devastation was everywhere.

The palm trees that were lined along the boulevard parallel to the Mediterranean had been bombed and shot. Once beautiful hotels and high rise apartments were blackened by fire and bombing with different sections blown off. A few windows of the hotel still had blinds clinging to the window frames.

The hotels were deserted and blackened. Burnt auto car frames clattered the streets. It had been one thing to see it on TV but another thing to be there.

While one section of the city looked like a bombed out ghost town, a block away, and people would be living a pathetic existence in a half bombed-out apartment with parts of their outside walls missing. Children played in rubble while the women hung clothing on a line stretched across the apartment balconies. The women kept busy by sweeping the streets and sidewalks as they chatted with one another.

Driving through the middle of Beirut, we were seeing some of the worst of it when we came to the "Green line." The "Green line" was a dividing line that ran through the city dividing East and West Beirut. The west section of Beirut was predominantly Muslim. The airport, the American embassy, the University and many of the hotels were all in West Beirut.

East Beirut was predominantly Christian and I was told it was ruled by Christian militia. Ashrafieh, where we were going, is located on the highest hill in Beirut. It was somewhat secluded from the rest of this city. In a way, it had a society all its own with churches and parochial schools.

As we drove up to the Farah's (Omars parents) apartment, I was glad to see their building intact. Outside of the Farah's apartment, several people were waiting to greet us. As we walked up the stairs and into their apartment, more people were inside.

Family, including many aunts, uncles, and cousins, friends and neighbors filled the room. Everyone took their turn to greet us. It had been a year since they had seen Omar, and they were excited to see him, again and meet his American fiancé.

Aside from Omar's brother Robert, who had lived in Paris, there were his parents, his oldest brother Maroon, his wife Nadia and their daughter Ahlena, his other two brothers Pierre and Simon and his sister Sarah, and a large group of uncles, aunts and cousins. It was overwhelming at first but I came to know them all.

Arabic coffee, tea and pastries were offered to everyone and as all the hellos and introductions were made, I sat down and began to establish who everyone was.

For the next few days, people continued to stop in to see Omar and meet me. Looking back, I think our being there in Beirut brought everyone a little hope that things would improve once again in Beirut. That people would return, even if it was only for a visit.

A Day on the Mediterranean

VERY EARLY ONE morning, Omar and I drove to his uncle's apartment to pick him up and go fishing. Omar's uncle lived in predominately but not exclusive, Muslim sector. Although it was still dark, I could see the bombed buildings and the rubble on the street.

His uncle Paul was ready and waiting for us, just having made a pot of Arabic coffee which we quickly drank before we left.

The streets were empty during the fifteen minute drive. We saw no one on the street, but then, it was early dawn. Once we got to the best fishing spot, we walked along the big rocks that jetted out into the beautiful Mediterranean. I was very windy and cold making the water choppy and as the water crashed onto the rocks a cold spray of water hit us.

Behind us, the sun began to rise over the range of mountains behind us, painting the sky with vibrant colors and the sun bringing some warmth to the air. The fish were biting and it wasn't long before we had plenty of fish for dinner.

Occasionally I would try fishing, but was more interested in exploring the rocks and looking at the sea urchins that were on the rocks under the water. The water was clear and the sea urchins were vibrant colors of yellow, purple, red, pink, and green. They were round with soft spikes and when put in your hand, they would slowly move.

The sea urchins attached themselves to the sides of the rocks. Cracking one open, Omar told me to eat it. Similar to mustard in color and texture, they were very tasty but almost to pretty to eat.

After counting the fish, they decided they had enough and gathered up the fishing poles and cooler and we headed back home.

It was such a beautiful day that we decided to spend the day on the Mediterranean swimming and sunbathing by the sea. Omar had a friend who had given us an open invitation to use his chalet up the coast from Beirut giving us the opportunity of having the beach to ourselves and relax.

The chalet was charming and had all the comforts of home. On the way, we had stopped at the market and picked up some fruit and vegetables. Omar brought some of the fish he had caught that morning and he cooked the fish as I made a salad with the vegetables, saving the fruit for dessert. We relaxed on the patio enjoying our meal and the tranquility as well as the beauty of the sea.

Later in the afternoon, we began to hear explosions in the distance which only meant that somewhere, not too far way, fighting was going on. Billows of dark smoke would appear creating ugly, black clouds in the clear, blue sky.

War would soon become a reality that I would have to accept during my time in Lebanon. There would be days though, like our day on the Mediterranean, when we could, if only for a time, enjoy the beauty of the day.

The Mountain

I T WAS ONE of those days that stay with you forever. The day began as a beautiful, warm, spring day. I sat on the balcony outside of the Farah's house in my Mickey Mouse T-shirt enjoying a cup of tea. Beirut was quiet and the people seemed to feel some of the tranquility in the air. It was hard to believe that not far from us, fighting was going on.

A picnic had been planned for the family and me. We were to have shish-ka-bob on top of one of their favorite mountains. After the food was prepared, we gathered everything and everyone together and started our journey.

As we got out of Beirut, we started up a range of mountains. The scenery, the smell of the pine trees and the twists in the road reminded me of New England. For a country so old and small, much of the area looked untouched.

Before we reached the top, I could see why this mountain with its spectacular view, was so special. For miles you could see mountains cascading in the distance. There was an area of grass dotted with wildflowers and pine trees. Except for us, no one was around.

While we were setting everything up, Omar's mother started to tell me about one of her favorite writers. She said that Kahlil Gibran (who's writing I've always loved) was from one of the mountains around us.

She seemed both pleased and surprised to learn that I not only knew who he was but was excited to learn more about him. Finally, we had found something in common, a connection.

While the shish-ka-bob was cooking on the grill, we looked for a special kind of pine cone. The trees in this area have pine cones that have soft seeds inside them and are used in many recipes. Before long, we had plenty of pine nuts and supper was ready.

The food and surroundings couldn't have been better. Everyone was happy and relaxed. While most of us continued with our meal, Omar's brother Simon had taken a walk when he suddenly screamed for us. I couldn't understand what he was saying, but I could hear the urgency in his voice.

Maroon quickly ran over and we began to follow. Nestled between two pine trees was the decaying body of a soldier. It almost seemed as if it had been placed there, face up. A fine layer of dirt covered the man's body.

Insects had infested different areas of the body. Dried blood on his shirt and the open wound in the center of his chest was evidence as to how the soldier probably died.

Parts of the soldier's face and hands exposed layers of skin that had been eaten away or had decayed revealing bones. His khaki clothes appeared to have been eaten away by moths. Flies hovered over the body like vultures. A pungent smell like bad meat lingered in the area.

Maroon was certain it was an enemy soldier. Omar mumbled something I didn't understand, while one of the younger brothers cursed and kicked dirt on the body, another one spit on what remained of the man. I was horrified and began to cry. Only then did I begin to understand the hatred after years of war.

The corpse before us was an MIA, another casualty of war that didn't come home. I wondered about the man, who was he? Was his family still waiting for him? Did he die all alone? Why was he still there?

My thoughts briefly drifted back to a few years before when so many American MIAs did not come back from Vietnam. My mind was a blur and I felt sick. I walked away, feeling numb. We had all become solemn and soon left. I was grateful the ride back was quiet. It was weeks before I could close my eyes without seeing the body.

An Emotional Day

OMAR WAS BECOMING more comfortable in Beirut and didn't want to return to Paris. He told me that he had been thinking about making a life for us in Beirut. Omar wanted to reopen his tailor shop and begin again.

After telling me, I became very upset and began to cry. I was not happy about the idea of staying in Lebanon. Ahlena was sitting next to me in the car and handed me her doll for comfort.

Maroon and Nadia were taking Ahlena, Omar and I out for the day. As we drove through the different sectors of Beirut, I noticed the many women in mourning who were wearing black clothing. I watched as a teenage boy who had lost his leg, hobbled by on his crutches. Battle scars were everywhere.

The Lebanese people appeared to be determined that life, even during a war, must go on. Men still gathered outside of shops smoking hubbly bubblies or playing chess. A vendor was selling orange juice and lemonade from fresh squeezed fruit.

We stopped at a busy open air market that sold everything from live chickens, assorted seafood and produce to various household items and gold jewelry. The market was surrounded by bombed out buildings that were once a very prosperous part of the city filled with cafes, clothing stores and nightclubs.

Omar and Maroon had lost a cousin and a close family friend both killed in the war. We went to visit the families to pay our respect. Even in their grief, their Lebanese hospitability never wavered.

Although the day had been a difficult one emotionally, Omar still talked of staying in Beirut. He wanted to be married when Robert would be in Lebanon for a visit. I loved Omar but I could not find peace with his decision. Only the future would change Omar's mind.

The Confrontation

THE EVENING WAS warm and the city of Beirut was quiet and at peace. Omar had borrowed Maroon's car so he could go for a drive. Omar drove high up into one of the pine covered mountain ranges. We found a pretty spot to pull off the side of the road.

From where we were parked, we could look down from the mountain and see the city of Beirut. Beyond Beirut was the beautiful Mediterranean Sea. The moon was bright and full and its reflection danced across the water while the stars twinkled in the sky.

Omar and I had just been there long enough to smoke a cigarette before we had company. Suddenly, a jeep with four Syrian soldiers pulled directly in front of Samir's car. They jumped out of the jeep and quickly surrounded us with their machine guns aimed at us.

We were ordered out of the car and two soldiers were ordered to search the car for drugs or any ammunition while the soldier apparently in charge, questioned us. A fourth soldier remained in front of us holding his machine gun aimed to towards us.

As a peacekeeping force, one of the Syrian soldier's responsibilities was to police different areas and enforce the curfew. The Syrians had a reputation of not being fond of the Christian Lebanese. Evidently, one soldier saw Omar smoking a cigarette and threw the butt out of the window.

"Were you smoking hashish?" he asked angrily.

"No," Omar replied.

"Are you Muslims?" the soldier asked.

"We are Christians," Omar replied as I nodded in agreement.

"What sector are you from?" he continued. Growing impatient, the soldier glanced at the other two soldiers searching the car.

"Ashrafieh", answered Omar.

The more questions he asked, the more nervous I became. We had crossed over the green line. As Christians, we were in the wrong area and had violated the curfew. After curfew, Christians and Muslims must stay in their own sectors.

"What are you doing here?" the soldier asked Omar.

"We were just going for a drive." Omar answered. For years, Omar would drive through the mountain ranges never worrying about the time or the area. But, the war had changed all that. I could sense that Omar was getting very nervous and tense which scared me; especially with the fourth soldier staring at us and never lowering his rifle.

"Let me see your passports," he demanded. When he saw mine, he was surprised.

"An American, what are you doing here?" The soldier asked. Omar told them that we were engaged and we had come to Lebanon for me to meet his family.

When the search of the car turned up nothing, the two soldiers were ordered to search the ground area around the car. My heart raced in fear.

"What did they want from us?" I thought to myself. The soldier in charge started to speak to me and I said I spoke very little Arabic. Scared to death and fearing we would be shot, I prayed and thought about my family and the good 'ole USA. I wished I was there.

As the two soldiers continued to comb the area, the soldier in charge handed us our passports. It seemed like hours since the confrontation had begun. The soldiers told us to go back to where we belonged. The two soldiers were told to stop looking, since the search turned up nothing. As quickly as they came, they left.

Very shaken by the whole incident, we were thankful it was over and had ended peacefully. We decided we had had enough excitement for one night. Omar drove us back to his parents' apartment where Omar told his family about our experience.

I think it was the first time Omar accepted the fact that Beirut would never be the same again. The only way to be safe and to have a peaceful life would be to leave Beirut.

The Reality of War

T HERE WAS ONE day that stays in my mind and I can still look back with regret. It was a beautiful spring day; the warm breeze blew the spring air throughout the house. It was Palm Sunday, and except for Omar and me, the rest of the family went to church. Omar's family had asked me if I wanted to go and I didn't.

The truth was, I was afraid to go. Christians were still being killed in and around the city and I thought the church would be an easy target. Fear had begun to dominate my life. Church services were held without an incident and Pierre brought home a large, green, palm branch, a symbol of hope.

I told Pierre how I had wanted to go but that I had been afraid. Pierre said he understood and for a while we stood on the small balcony, off the kitchen, overlooking the shattered city. We talked about his fear of living in a country torn apart by war. The devastation was a constant reminder. What a pathetic life for anyone to live with.

The war had affected everyone and I was upset that I could do nothing to help change their situation. I had come to love Omar's family and cared deeply about many of the people I had met during my time in Beirut.

The war was drawing closer. As Omar, uncle Paul and I sat on the curb on the street by the Farah's home, we could hear gunfire in the distance. Omar and Paul tried to ignore it as I wrote in the dirt with a stick.

Everyone knew the war was getting closer to Beirut and they tried to shelter me from hearing about it. The American Embassy had closed after having had both a skeleton staff and limited hours. As an American, I should have left when the embassy closed.

If I ever felt like I was in a hopeless situation before, I realized that was nothing, it was now. No one had much money, so no one could leave Beirut for a safer place. I was beginning to understand a little better about how hard it was to know a war would soon be coming to your neighborhood and yet you couldn't do anything to stop it or get away from it.

Night time became more and more difficult for me. At night, I would lay awake for a long time listening for any strange noises outside, or for the sound of any one trying to break in. As I was lying in bed trying to sleep, this same scenario played my mind almost every night

I would hear the Syrian soldiers coming up the stairs in the apartment building. From one apartment to the next, someone would be shouting orders and then there would be screaming and gunfire as the soldiers eventually worked their way up to the Farah's.

Breaking down the door they would begin shooting everyone. I would be in the kitchen kneeling on the floor begging for my life. But like everyone else in the building I would be shot too.

My heart would always be pounding fast and hard in my chest. Looking back, I don't think I had gotten over the fear of the confrontation. I was scared and there was little anyone could do to ease my fear.

My only hope for leaving Beirut was by asking my dad for money. I was lucky to get a phone line out of Beirut. My mom was ecstatic to know I was OK. The news had reported that hundreds of Christians have been killed in and around Beirut. They had not heard from me since my arrival in Lebanon and they feared the worst. My dad was relieved but understandably furious. Why was I still there?

I tried to explain the situation and apologized for worrying them. My dad agreed to send the money and when the money arrived, we went to get our visas and tickets to Paris. It was then that I was determined to do what I could to get the family out of Beirut. I had no idea how, but once again, I thought about the voice I had heard and knew I would not be doing it alone.

A Wedding in the Village

O NCE IN A while, there were those days when you never thought about the war and just enjoyed yourself. This was one of those days.

The day started early. We all got dressed for a long day that began at the bride-to-be's house. All invited guests brought gifts and visited the bride before the wedding. When we arrived, the house was already full of people, gifts, food and drinks. It was like a reception before the ceremony, complete with everything but the groom and the wedding cake. When all the invited guests arrived, they escorted the soon-to-be bride to the church.

The church was in a village in one of the mountains. It was a long drive to the church, but the scenery was beautiful. Everyone followed the lead car in their cars and beeped their horns. As we started driving up the mountain, I looked down the twisting road and saw the long caravan of cars. It was an incredible sight. It looked like half the city had been invited.

The further up into the mountains, the more beautiful it became. The narrow winding road was bordered with pine and other trees. Nestled in between the trees were beautiful villas with white limestone walls and steep red/orange tile roofs. It was so pretty it looked like a painting. Everything looked too perfect and in place to be real.

By the time we reached the top the church bells were ringing. The village was alive with laughter and excitement. The church was packed and over-flowing, so a few of us had to wait outside. That gave me a chance to walk around and check out the view.

The church was at the top of this mountain range and a few yards from the church parking lot was a view of the cascading mountains below. I think I could have lived in a place like that forever.

After the ceremony were the greetings to the newlyweds. The people began to leave to go to the reception up the road. The house was huge and beautiful. The whole top floor had a balcony around it. People were everywhere. There were tables of food. If they didn't have it, you didn't need it.

The music, dancing, eating and gaiety went on for hours. Before the bride and groom were to change and leave, Omar and I, somehow, were chosen to stand on the balcony and throw down rose petals on the couple. I didn't even know the couple yet I had this honor. I've thought of that day many times since then. It was truly a beautiful wedding.

Where Do the Children Play?

THE WAR AND the stress it caused were really affecting every one. Tempers were flaring, frustration over the present and future outlook only depressed everyone. Because of the occasional gunfire, people stayed at home or at least close by. Everyone was feeling cooped up. Nadia asked me to take a walk and a much needed break from the discussions of the war. She was tired of the changes and restrictions that the war put on everyone's lifestyle.

Earlier in the day, I had heard the song "Where Do the Children Play?" by Cat Stevens. That song played it in my mind as Nadia and I were walking. Nadia and I walked to a small store where she bought us a Coke. We talked in Arabic and gestures since I knew very little Arabic and Nadia spoke no English. But, we managed to get out points across.

Every day the people in Beirut had to overcome their fear to just venture outside and walk down their own street. They had to have faith to believe in tomorrow and a determination to pick up the pieces and go on.

Along the road by a building that had been bombed were beautiful flowers that looked like daisies. The colors were vibrant yellows, blues, lavender and red. They almost seemed out of place among the busted up concrete and dirt that had taken the place of grass and trees. From the street we were on, we could look down at the streets, houses and destruction below.

I wondered about the children of Beirut, or any war. Where do the children play? Nadia's daughter Ahlena couldn't run through the grass and flowers without stepping on debris or shattered glass and there were no parks anymore.

Instead of the energetic running around and curiosity of a two-year-old exploring the world around her, Ahlena had to spend days at a time in a dark, crowded, basement with a family and other neighbors to seek shelter from the gunfire and bombings.

Life in Beirut, as it was before the war, was gone and in the process children experienced a loss of innocence.

In the distance, below the street we were on, was a little boy about eight or nine years old. He was standing on a mound of dirt surrounded by rubble which was once an apartment building. He seemed too small for the fatigues he was wearing. He appeared to be standing guard as he held the rifle almost as big as he was.

Unfortunately, he wasn't playing with his buddies or playing with a toy gun. It was not uncommon for a young boy to take up a gun and help protect his family, especially if his father or brothers had been shot or killed.

How sad his reality couldn't be a game he was playing and if he grew tired of it, he could stop playing it and go play ball or fly a kite. I wish I could have sent him off to a better place where he could run free and just be a kid instead of a little soldier.

Nahida

O MAR HAD A friend named George whose girlfriend, Nahida had planned a picnic and a day at the sea. We picked Nahida up at her parent's apartment and she brought even more food to our already full basket of assorted food.

The weather was warm with a clear, blue sky. The sun caused the calm Mediterranean to sparkle. A warm breeze blew giving relief to the hot sun. It was a perfect day for swimming and lying in the sun. I was surprised when Nahida took off her dress and was wearing a bikini, not common attire in Beirut at that time. We stayed on the shore for most of the day.

Nahida had gone to college in England and aside from being fluent in English, she was well educated and very open minded. Her boyfriend George was a Christian and Nahida was a Muslim. But to her, being a Muslim was her faith and not her culture. She considered herself a modern Lebanese woman. She did not judge people by their faith or culture, but by what kind of person they were. Religion was something we never discussed.

Nahida and I easily slipped into a good friendship and the four of us got together often. We both enjoyed reading, especially at the beach and since most of her books were printed in English, she would give me a book when she was finished reading it.

Nahida and I spent hours talking about traveling, current affairs and life in America versus life in Lebanon. We would talk like old friends about almost anything. I enjoyed our time together. It was an easy, relaxed, friendship.

She usually worked in the morning and had the afternoons free. One day we had a day just for the two of us and we went to our favorite café. Later, we went to her apartment and she introduced me to waxing my legs. I did not like that very much. It was painful and my legs were red for two days. But I only had to do it once a month so. The pain was worth it, considering how long it lasted.

Towards the end of my time in Beirut, we saw very little of each other because of the fighting. Nahida did not live close to the Farahs and people stayed close to home, rarely going out for long. Nahida added a lot to my time in Beirut as well as showing me that cultural and religious differences did not have to come between friendships.

Silent Night

SLEEP HADN'T COME easily to me in the past 2 months. At night, I would stay awake and listen for any noise. By staying in Beirut, I had learned to fear war. Every day brought the threat of war getting closer. Two hundred Christians were killed by enemy soldiers in the mountains visible from our balcony, only days before.

One evening, I began to hear gunfire in the distance. The gunfire seemed to be getting closer and then it was silent. A few minutes later there was a noise that sounded like people shuffling around outside. A loud explosion shook the apartment. Gunfire was loud and constant.

Scared, I got up from my bed and slid under it. I had remembered what a Vietnam veteran had said to me about his escape from gunfire, while in a building. "I got away from the outside wall because a powerful rifle can shoot through concrete. Crawling to stay low, I found an area surrounded by inner walls." Remembering this, I quickly crawled out from under the bed towards the hall outside of the bedroom.

From the floor I reached up to Omar on his bed and tried to wake him up. When I told him to move to a safer place he told me the gunfire was nothing to worry about; to go back to sleep. Safely in the hall, I went into the living room to wake Omar's parents. They were sleeping on beds placed at opposite walls.

A table with wooden figurines on top of it was placed in the middle of the room between the two beds. Neither of Omar's parents woke up. I went into the room where Pierre, Sarah, and Simon slept. All of them were sleeping and safe. It was hard to believe they could sleep through the noise.

Shaking in fear, I sat down and cried as I prayed. The noise was so loud; I covered my ears with my hands. Finally, the gunfire began to get further away until it was too far away to hear anymore. When it remained quiet for a while, I got up from the floor and went back to bed, eventually drifting off to sleep.

The next morning, Pierre's loud cries of "Look at this!" and "Here's another one!" woke me up. Hearing their voices in the front room, I grabbed a robe and quickly went to join them. Maroon was heading through the front door with Nadia and Ahlena behind him. They wanted to make sure everyone was unharmed.

The Farahs were examining the bullet holes that riddled the walls. One of the carved wooden statues was on the floor, having been pierced by a stray bullet. They were all amazed everyone in the house slept through it all.

"There was a lot of gunfire and noise last night!" I said. Everyone in the room stopped talking and looked at me.

"I got up out of bed. I went crazy! I tried to wake you, but you went back to sleep. I stayed in the hall where I felt safe until it was over. I didn't know what else to do," I said in Lebanese. Standing closest to me was Mrs. Farah. We were both crying and we reached out and hugged each other.

Maroon then told us that the balcony had been blown off the apartment next door. Part of the outside wall to their front room was gone. Omar and his father went out on the balcony checking out the damage of their neighbor's house. Maroon kept telling everyone not to worry. We all knew he was as worried as the rest of us.

The Farahs in turn, told me it was something they had to live with. Families must continue to go on with their lives. Neighbors and friends came in and out of the apartment throughout the day making sure everyone was unharmed. No one in the neighborhood had been killed or injured during the shooting which had been a miracle in itself.

War. A simple little word that brings nothing but ugliness into people's lives.

Hassahn

NOT LONG AFTER I had met just about everyone I was to meet in Beirut, I met Hassahn. Before I met him, I had heard a lot about him. Never was an unkind or negative word spoken of him. When people spoke of Hassahn, the women often made the sign of the cross and raised their eyes as if in prayer. The men nodded in agreement. I was looking forward to meeting him.

As a child, Hassahn had grown up with these people and had been a childhood friend of Omar and his older brothers, Maroon and Robert. Omar's mother was like a second mother to him and he was like a son to her.

One day, as a group of us were visiting in the front room, we heard commotion in the front hall. "Hassahn!" the children shouted. Everyone rose from their seats to greet him with hugs and kisses. The love they had for this man brought tears to my eyes. They quickly offered him food and something to drink.

As I watched him, I was impressed by how he and his presence made it a festive occasion. Hassahn was tall with dark brown hair and light brown eyes. His rimmed glasses gave him a scholarly appearance. He was quiet and shy, but he liked to smile and when he did, it was contagious. He seemed embarrassed that everyone was making such a fuss over him.

Omar and I saw Hassahn on several occasions in Beirut. He spoke English very well which made it a lot easier to get to know him. One evening, Hassahn came over to the Farah's apartment and we had decided to go out for a walk and a breath of fresh air. The evening was warm and the sky was clear. Peace reigned in Beirut and it was very quiet.

Although it was early, the streets were empty. Hassahn, Omar and I were walking through that heavily bombed section of Beirut. An apartment building had been leveled by bombing leaving debris scattered over the sidewalk and street. The devastation caused by the war, left the area looking like a trash dump. A big rat ran in front of us and into the debris causing us to stop momentarily. The sight of the rat caused me to shiver.

"How can you stand to live here?" I asked Hassahn.

"I have no choice. I'd like to leave Beirut. It's very hard to live through a war. The war goes on and on, peace does not last long," Hassahn said.

"Where would you go if you could leave"? I asked.

"Canada," he replied without hesitation. "But it would be hard to get a visa to go there. I have no family in Canada. I have an aunt and uncle in the States though."

"You don't want to go to America?" I asked.

"No, I've heard many things about America, but I've never been impressed by what I've heard," he said in a factual manner."I hope you can leave Beirut some day," I replied. The thought of a good man like Hassahn not being able to leave Beirut made me feel sad. Even though I couldn't leave

Beirut because of a lack of money, I knew that I would have the option to leave. Many of the citizens of Beirut had no place else to go and had no way or money to get there if they could go.

During times of heavy fighting between Christians and Muslims, water and food supplies had been cut off from the Christian sector. Hassahn, a Muslim, would sneak across the green line at night and bring families food and water.

Hassahn also gave them hope gave them hope that they would survive those horrible times. He risked his life every time he did it. As often as he could, Hassahn took care of his friends and their families.

"To many people, you are a hero," I said.
"It took a lot of courage to do what you did."
"You risked your life to help so many people." Hassahn just shrugged his shoulders.

"I only did what I had to do. I love them, they are like my family." Many people told me that Hassahn was always helping anyone who needed it. That was a part of Hassahn that made him so special. The last time I heard, Hassahn was somewhere safe in the USA.

Because of my admiration for Hassahn, I found it hard to be objective; for like everyone else, he must have had his faults. But this much I can say, if we all had a little of Hassahn in us, there would be no more war.

Beirut, The Final Farewell

O N OUR LAST full day in Beirut, Omar's father took us to a restaurant for a farewell dinner that was right in the middle of paradise. It was one of the most beautiful places I have ever seen.

The restaurant was tucked away in a wooded area. Outside of the restaurant was a patio with tables where most of the patrons sat; but we were at a table a little further down from it. Not far from us was a wide running stream.

The water was crystal clear and it raced over the rocks making small waterfalls. Next to the stream was a carpet of green grass with wildflowers scattered here and there.

Surrounding us where tall trees that made a dome with their branches and leaves high above us. When the wind blew through the trees, you could see the blue sky as the sun filtered through. It was a haven, and I felt safe and protected against anything going on outside of that place.

There was a feast of assorted fish, meats, vegetables, fruits and desserts. The food was as delicious as the scenery was beautiful. We had a toast to our future and then a reminisced over our past three months together in Lebanon.

Omar's father told me of his fear that as an American, I would marry his son, take him to America and leave him. He had a friend whose son had married an American woman and a few years later, she walked out on both her husband and their daughter. I assured him that I wasn't going to marry Omar just to end up walking out on him.

For a while we talked about our plans and dreams. More than anything, I had needed that day to relax and reflect on both the good and bad experiences I had encountered while in Lebanon. I needed to find a kind of peace again.

As much as I was glad to leave the war in Lebanon, I was sorry to have to say goodbye to so many people I had come to care about. It was difficult for me knowing that while I was going to a safer place, everyone else had to stay and endure the war. I didn't have much to pack since I had given many of my clothes to Therese. I hate goodbyes; I get choked up and start crying.

Omar and I didn't know if we would ever see anyone again which made it even harder but, we told them, we would call them and keep in touch. Samir took us to the airport and left soon after we said goodbye.

Security had been tightened during my stay in Beirut and the airport had been closed and reopened several times due to fighting. I was thankful it was open when we needed it.

The airport was packed with people desperately trying to leave. I held my tickets so tightly, my knuckles turned white. It was not until Omar and I were on the plane and it had taken off that I could sit back and relax.

Beneath us was Lebanon, a country scarred and ripped apart by war. I didn't want to look back at Lebanon, my memories and experiences there would have to be enough. I was grateful for the time and experiences I had had in Lebanon and thanked God I had left the country alive.

Through Omar and our experiences I had met many diverse people. I had met other Christians, Lebanese and Palestinian, Muslims, Druze and Jews. They all had their stories to tell, their burdens to carry. I can't say anyone was totally right or totally wrong. Everyone was strong in their own beliefs.

The more I learned about these different people, the more alike they seemed. They all had family, and friends; they laughed, cried and had dreams and fears just like everyone else. The one common bond they all shared was that of misunderstanding and discrimination in one way or another. All of them had been touched or affected by war.

One of the saddest things to me was that religion separated people and divided nations rather than bringing everyone together. But then God did not make religions. He gave us rules to live by. I was glad for the opportunity to meet these different people and hear their stories.

If I failed to learn anything or pass anything along about some of them, I missed an opportunity in my life to share the belief that all lives are precious, even those of our adversaries. Until we respect other people's rights for their beliefs and their ways, we will never have a chance for peace on Earth.

Chapter 4

Another Turn in the Road

Paris after Beirut

I WAS RELIEVED when our plane landed in Paris. It seemed like it had been a lot longer than three months in Beirut. As soon as we arrived in the airport terminal, I called my parents to let them know we had arrived safely.

Omar and I found a place to stay in the Latin Quarter of Paris, where we had stayed before. At night I had no problem sleeping, knowing it was safe, something that had been so hard for me to do in Beirut.

Coming back to Paris from Beirut was a culture shock. I was walking down the street when a car backfired, sounding like an explosion. I jumped in terror thinking, momentarily, I was in Beirut. My nerves were shot.

I was reminded of the time in Beirut when a car backfired and a group of teenagers panicked until they realized it was just a car. The images of war and the people we left behind, were on my mind. I wanted to do something to help them, but first I had to go to America.

One important thing about my going to Lebanon was that I had been there, seen it, lived it and experienced living in a war zone. Before going there, I could only imagine what it was like and how it had affected the people. The experience had given me a better understanding of what it must have been like to live through a war.

As much as Omar hated leaving both his family and Lebanon, he was glad to be back in Paris. At least there was peace and a better chance of a normal life. But I could also understand how hard it was for Omar to leave the country he had loved.

Now that we were back in Paris, I could start filling out forms for our marriage license. Medical tests had been completed so we submitted all the papers and forms. Hopefully, we could be married in a couple of weeks. There wouldn't be a lot to plan since we were to be married in the court house.

Robert would be out of town so two of our friends, Gerhardt and Melany were standing up for us. The important thing was to get married. After we were married, we could begin to process Omar's papers for his immigration to the States. The process would start at the U.S. Embassy to submit forms for a green card.

In Lebanon, we had discussed our future plans and Omar agreed that moving to America to begin our new life would be the best decision for us.

Our Wedding Day

THE LONG-AWAITED DAY had finally arrived. Beforedws the alarm went off, I got out of bed and opened the big, French window. The morning sun began to peek through the clouds. It was early, so the streets were still quiet.

Robert was out of town on business, but he had given us a key to his apartment so I could have the morning to myself to get ready for the big day. It was nice to be able to take a shower in the privacy of Robert's apartment, instead of going down the hall of the hotel to a bathroom that was for everyone. I took a long, hot shower and then combed and dried my long hair.

I sat on the edge of the opened window as I drank a cup of tea and listened to my Mood Blues record. The sun was playing hide and seek with the clouds and it looked as if I would be having a rainy wedding day as the weather man had predicted. Thinking about the day ahead, I was lost in thought when the doorbell rang.

The delivery man presented me with a big, white box with a ribbon and a bow around it. Inside the box was a beautiful bouquet of thirteen budding red roses, just beginning to reveal the lovely petals.

The thirteenth rose was for good luck. Picking up the bouquet, I smelled the wonderful fragrance of the roses that was surrounded with baby's' breath. The bouquet added the final touch to my wedding.

I carefully placed the roses on the coffee table and picked up my overnight bag. The bag contained a recent letter from my dad, a silver charm bracelet from my brothers, my mom's hanky, a borrowed hair clip from a friend, and a blue crocheted shawl my mom had made for me. I placed everything on a table by the closet where I had hung the wedding gown from Robert.

Our wedding was set for 2:00 in the afternoon. I got dressed and for the final touch I put on the perfume Omar had given me on my first day in Paris. I hadn't been dressed for long when Omar came to the door dressed in his suit. He looked so handsome. Until then, I hadn't been nervous. We left the apartment to walk to the City Hall.

As we were walking, a light rain fell from the sky. I wasn't going to let a little rain ruin my day. As we walked down the narrow Paris streets, people would turn and look at us, wave and shout greetings and best wishes. I was so happy I barely noticed the rain.

Gerhardt and Melanie were there and together we went in the room to meet the judge. The judge greeted us warmly, complimenting me on my dress. He told me I made a beautiful bride.

The ceremony, of course, was in French. Speaking very little French, the judge let me know when to say, "I do." I felt something was missing by not understanding what the judge was saying. But I had been to enough weddings to know what was said.

After the ceremony, the four of us went back to Gerhardt's apartment where we had cake, champagne and some French food. We stayed for a couple hours celebrating the day. Afterwards, Omar and I left to change and meet some other friends, who had to work and missed the ceremony,

We joined them on the Champs Elysees where we sat in a café. They treated us to dinner and a few drinks. We were broke, but also happy and in love. Having a honeymoon in Paris was like a dream come true.

Bubba Paul

THERE WERE TIMES in Paris when we would go for days wondering where our next meal was coming from. I had spent the last of the money I had brought with me. Fortunately for us, there were people like Bubba Paul who would help us out.

Bubba Paul was an older man in his sixties. Once you met him, you'd recognize him on the street because he always wore the same beret and carried his small black leather shoulder bag. He was a small man and the years had caused his back and shoulders to curve and hunch which made him appear even shorter. He spoke only Arabic and French, so we spoke very little to one another.

When we were down on our luck, it seemed we would turn a corner and there was Bubba Paul. He would buy us a meal making sure we had enough to eat and drink and then give Omar some money. Sometimes he would invite us to his apartment where he would feed us and find Omar some kind of work to do. He knew a lot of people in Paris both French and Lebanese.

One of the jobs are Bubba Paul found for us was making special drapes for a woman he knew. These weren't ordinary drapes either. They had special pleats and the huge room they were made for had eight huge ceiling to floor windows.

Omar found a good job as a tailor. Bubba Paul introduced me to a man he knew from Cairo who had a stall where he sold imported merchandise including leather pocketbooks, belts, jewelry, shirts, blouses, skirts, incense and holders, as well as small knickknacks. The man offered me a job

I had to get up early to help Eli set up the stall and take it down at night. Certain streets and areas permitted a person to sell their wares between a shop and the street, but allowing enough room on the sidewalk for people to walk. We had neighbors on both sides of our stand and it was a common sight in Paris.

As far as I knew, Bubba Paul had no family of his own. But almost everyone I met who was Lebanese knew him and affectionately called him Bubba Paul. Bubba was the word for father in Lebanese. A few other people told me Bubba Paul had helped them also.

Bubba Paul was very kind to me and sometimes he would have a small token gift for me. Once when we were in Beirut we met with him and he gave me some French perfume and bath oils.

The last time we saw him was after Omar and I were married, and we would soon be leaving for the States. He bought us an elaborate dinner in celebration. I hugged him and thanked him for all he had done for us. He looked me in the eyes and smiled at me as if I had just given him a special gift.

Good Morning America, How Are Ya?

N O MATTER HOW much I loved Paris, I wanted to go home. My travels in Paris and Beirut had not always been easy; exciting at times, but difficult. I had met many people; some of them had become friends; although they would only be part of my life for a short time, they had made my life fuller with their friendship.

Paris would always be a dream come true even with the hard times. But Paris wasn't home. I loved America too much to be away for too long. I was happy when I ran into Americans in Paris.

Unless I walked, the Metro was the only way to travel in Paris. As a matter of fact, I like taking the Metro. Except for getting lost a few times and the crowds, I never had a problem.

The snacks in the Metro station's vending machines were the cheapest around, so when I had some spare change I would treat myself to an occasional candy bar.

It was not uncommon to see and hear a lot of fellow Americans in the Metro stations which was another thing that appealed to me. Many young people were seen with their backpacks as they were touring Europe.

Periodically, they would have a guitar or some other instrument and would sing while people walked by to earn a little extra money. No big deal, street musicians can be found in many cities, but to a homesick American, they were a little bit of home.

There was one man who usually sang in the Metro station by the American Embassy. He frequently sang the song, The City of New Orleans. If I had the time, I hung around until he finished it or would wait until he sang it again if he was singing something else. He was a good singer, but he was no Arlo Guthrie. But I was always looking for him just the same.

His singing always made me feel better, except for one time when I had just left the embassy and was told Omar's immigration would take a lot longer than I had expected, because of all the red tape. So as I went down to the Metro, there the man was singing my song and I started to cry. I just wanted to go home.

I never talked to my Metro minstrel, but I thank him for making my day a little brighter so many times. When I heard this song on the radio after I did get back to the States, it never sounded quite as good as it had in Paris.

Alicia

AFTER WE WERE married, Omar began to work for a tailor shop making men's clothes. He had met another man about his age, Adnon, who was from Syria. His fiancé, Alicia, was an American from California. At seven months pregnant, she was well on her way to becoming a mother. She was nervous about having a baby in Paris without her family close by.

Alicia's parents were excited to have their first grandchild but they were upset that Alicia was pregnant and unmarried. Her fiancé was not in a hurry to marry her either, which concerned her. She would often say to me that as a married woman, I should be the one who was pregnant.

Several weeks after our wedding day, I had begun to feel different. I felt sick to my stomach and was lightheaded a lot. Crackers usually made me feel better but I was so tired. One day on my way to meet Alicia, I was walking down the stairs from our room when I slipped down the last few stairs. I was so dizzy; I sat there until my head stopped spinning.

At first I wasn't sure what was wrong with me but, after that fall I began to think I was pregnant. Wanting to be sure in case I was wrong, I kept it to myself for awhile. One day as Alicia and I were walking in town, I mentioned to her about how I had been feeling. She told me she had a feeling I was pregnant.

I made an appointment for the following day to see a doctor and Alicia went with me. The doctor confirmed I was pregnant. After telling Alicia, we both became excited and hugged one another. We had become good friends and Alicia and I were both looking forward to becoming mothers. Omar, to my delight, was thrilled.

Both Alicia and I were homesick. One day, the song Hotel California, by the Eagles played on the radio and Alicia began to cry. That night I told Omar that I wanted to go home as soon as we could.

Omar and I had discussed going to America after we were married, but now that Omar had a good job, he had second thoughts. Omar was thinking in the "now" and not considering the future of supporting a family. We could not continue to live in a hotel and an apartment would be expensive.

Alicia and Adnon were struggling to pay for their small apartment. How would it be when their baby was born? Alicia was now in her final weeks of pregnancy and was worried about money.

Thankfully, Robert and Marcel talked to Omar and set him straight. Staying in Paris would only continue to be a struggle. The embassy was working on Omar's papers and Robert felt that going to America was the best option for Omar and me.

Marcel

MARCEL WAS A boyhood friend of Omar. They were raised and grew up together in Beirut and remained close friends. Omar and Marcel were like brothers.

The first time I met Marcel was in a café on the Champs Elysee. I was surprised Marcel was Lebanese because of his green eyes and light brown hair. He spoke no French only English and German.

Marcel preferred Germany to France, but came to Paris often to see his friends. We would see him for days at a time and then he would go back to Germany. Like many other Lebanese, he was biding his time till he could go back to Lebanon.

Marcel was very familiar with Omar and my relationship, he was the friend who had read and translated my letters to Omar. Omar would then tell Marcel what to write and then Marcel helped Omar write and send a letter back to me. Since Middle Eastern writing looks like a type of shorthand written from right to left, it was good practice for Omar to write cursive from left to right.

Marcel was very helpful in teaching Omar to write English and had helped him learning English phrases. They spent a lot of time speaking to one another in Lebanese, but Marcel always made a point of speaking to me in English along with teaching me helpful Lebanese phrases.

I felt very comfortable around Marcel; he was usually very upbeat and liked to laugh. The three of us spent a lot of time together seeing the different sites in and around Paris, whether it was a museum in Paris or an abandoned castle outside of Paris.

Once when Omar and I were in Beirut Marcel surprised us with a visit. He went over to the Farahs shortly after he arrived and was surprised to see me there.

In Paris, when Marcel and I discussed my going to Lebanon, he did not think it was a good idea for us to go.

"I heard it is quiet in Beirut. Much of the fighting has stopped," I had said.

"There is still a civil war going on! Why do you think so many Lebanese are over here?" Marcel pointed out.

"The man at the Lebanese Embassy had said it was safe and the American Embassy is open," I said, trying to sound convincing. Besides, one of the best ways to learn more about someone is to meet with family and know more about their family and know where they came from," I stated.

"The Lebanon, now, is not the same country we grew up in! Omar should know that," Marcel sternly stated.

Marcel gave me a hug and asked how I was doing. Wanting Marcel to hear how I had picked up the language, I answered in Lebanese, "fine." I continued speaking to him in Lebanese for awhile.

"Learning the language," he said, "You speak very well," he added with a wink.

"Thanks", I said smiling. At that time, I had been to Lebanon over two months and I was anxious to leave. The American Embassy had closed and I had seen and experienced enough of a war situation to understand what many of the Lebanese in Paris had left behind as well as what the civilians had gone through and were still dealing with every day.

Marcel was encouraging Omar to leave Beirut soon. There was a lot of civil unrest and men were being kidnapped by the Syrians. The mere thought of being kidnapped upset Omar. Before Omar went to Paris, he was kidnapped by the Syrians who thought that Omar was a member of the Phalanges party.

Phalanges are people who are part of a fanatical religious group also known as Christian militia. Omar had been held for three days before his family and friends could convince Omar's captors that he was not who they thought he was.

After he had been released, Omar flew to Paris to be with Robert and be out of Lebanon. Marcel, Maroon and Hassahn was among the group of people dealing with his captors for Omar's release. Marcel had told me about Omar's capture soon after we met Paris. Later in Beirut, Maroon had told me about it. It was a subject that was not usually discussed.

One morning, Omar borrowed Maroon's car and we went over to Marcel's home. After meeting some of his family, the three of us spent the day driving to a mountain area, where time had come to a stop thousands of years ago. Along the way, we stopped and bought some fruit and fresh vegetables to eat during our drive. When we had arrived at the mountain range, I remember thinking that seeing this made the Amish seem modern.

It was like stepping back in time. The men in the fields wore robed clothes and sandals, carrying a stick to lean on, just as I could imagine shepherds with their sheep as they would have been in biblical times. Families lived in small dwellings, almost like huts and the farmers raised sheep and vegetables with various fruit trees that not only supplied fresh fruit, but offered shade from the hot sun when they were busy in the fields.

I was fascinated by how this part of the world lived. No phone lines, electric or plumbing. Big wells were seen with a bucket to bring up the water. A horse and cart seemed to be their only means of transportation.

As we continued to drive along the mountain ranges, it was an awesome site to see the large olive groves along with the fig, orange, lemon, and mulberry groves.

Much of Lebanon was flush with pine forests, almond bushes, acacia, poplar and sycamore trees. The giant Cedars of Lebanon were always a beautiful sight. After hours of driving, it was getting close to the curfew and we had to head back to civilization and drop Marcel off. We saw Marcel a few days later, before he left for Germany.

We spent time with Marcel on a few other occasions before our last visit with him. We met Marcel in the Latin Quarter of Paris and went to a restaurant on the Champs Elysee where Marcel would take us out to dinner. Omar and I were leaving Paris for America soon. Omar wanted to tell Marcel about my pregnancy, now that it had been confirmed by a doctor.

While we were walking by the Arc de Triumph, we saw a phone with a few people standing around it as if they were waiting their turn. Marcel knew I was hoping to call my parents, because of something I wanted to discuss with them, so he asked if they had an open line and they said they did.

Only one man was waiting to use the phone and we were in no hurry, Marcel told me to call home while they went to buy cigarettes and grab a coffee. I had never used the magic telephone in such a public place. When the last person got off the phone, he handed it to me and they all left.

It was afternoon in Paris making it morning in Baltimore. My mom was doing the morning dishes when I called. She was both glad and surprised to hear from me. As I talked to my mom, I looked down the famous boulevard and thought how lucky I had been to be in Paris, even though it wasn't always easy to live there.

I told my mom she was going to be a grandmother and we both cried with happiness and excitement. My mom said she had a dream that I was pregnant. I guess it was mother's intuition. Omar and Marcel came up the street as I was saying goodbye.

The last I heard, Marcel had moved to the States to join his brother in North Carolina and he had gotten married. I always smile when I think of him.

Time to say Goodbye

ON MY LAST few days in Paris I had time to reflect on how I felt when I first arrived. Then I had money in my pocket, I was full of dreams for Omar and I felt as if I could achieve almost anything.

So much had happened in the last several months and it was a lot to take in. Beirut had opened my eyes to a different culture and the experiences and memories had a big impact on me and that would never be forgotten.

I walked down the street towards the Fontaine St. Michele, purchased a cup of tea and a pastry and sat down on a bench to watch the people mulling around the square. I was remembering how excited I had been to be experiencing Paris. The busting city was so alive and the places to go seemed endless. I had been able to experience Paris as someone who lived there. It was hard at times but I loved it and the lifestyle. I savored the memories.

Now with a husband and a baby on the way, I was looking forward to settling down and raising a family. A whole new life was ahead of me but, it was time to move on, a time to say goodbye to Paris. My life was going to take me down an unexpected path.

Arriving in Baltimore

NOTHING MADE ME happier than arriving safely in the States. My parents picked us up from the airport and gave us both a warm welcome. It must have been difficult for them, but they didn't show it.

Before Omar, my parents knew who I was dating, but now, no matter what they thought of my choice, the decision was made. Omar spoke a little bit in the car when I wasn't asking about the latest news and what I had missed, my parents were asking me about my adventures of the last nine months.

The first few days were busy with Omar meeting my family and some close friends. Compared to Lebanon, America was a culture shock. Even though Omar had spent time in Paris, it was still different in the States and the language barrier would be difficult for a while.

Omar wanted to get a job as soon as possible and to his credit, he got a job three days after arriving in Baltimore. Omar had a job working in a large coat factory. His new boss would show Omar what needed to be done and Omar would do exactly what his boss wanted done.

Omar's boss was impressed by how well Omar accurately and quickly he sewed and got his job done. Omar was a good worker and his boss was very happy with both him and his work. Omar was also learning English quickly.

My parents were glad to have us stay with them and wanted us to live with them until our baby was born, giving us a chance to save up some money.

Robert called us frequently from Paris to keep in touch and hear how things were going. Robert also kept Omar informed on his family and any news from Beirut. Communication to Beirut was difficult because telephone lines were often down, and mail delivery wasn't always possible due to sporadic fighting. Robert's job enabled him to fly to Beirut frequently, keeping everyone informed of the latest news.

Omar settled in quickly and was happy that things were working out well. When we could, we would drive around Baltimore and see the sights. He got to know Baltimore and became more comfortable with the American way of life. Every day, we spent time working on his English. I was happy that Omar and my family were getting along.

Settling in

ONE DAY, MY dad's dental assistant was sick, so I filled in for her, one of his patients, Mrs. Prodey, had an appointment that day. During my time in Paris and Lebanon, my dad had kept her updated on my travels and marriage to Omar.

Mrs. Prodey was a retired English teacher who shared both my dad and my passion for traveling and different adventures. She was a widow in her seventies who was young at heart and had an enthusiasm for life that was contagious. I always looked forward to seeing her.

I had mentioned to her that I was trying to help Omar with his English when she told me about a class that she taught at night school for those whose second language was English. The two hour classes were held one evening a week at a local high school.

I mentioned the class to Omar and he had been interested in going. I told him I would go to the classes with him so we could review what Mrs. Prodey had gone over in class, during the week. Omar and I went every week until his English had improved enough for him to get a driver's license and he could drive himself to class.

Debbie's father had an old car he wasn't using that was just sitting in his driveway. Her father said if he could get it to run, he could drive it home.

Omar got the keys, turned it on and the engine ran fine. Omar now had a car to go with his license.

There were certain foods that Omar missed that could not be found in the supermarkets. One day as we were shopping in a mall, we came across a Lebanese deli. Omar was excited. As we entered the shop, the smell of coffee and spices surrounded us. The store contained Arabic coffee, spices, different meats, pita bread, assorted olives and chesses. Everything that Omar wanted was available in the store.

Noticing Omar's obvious excitement, we were offered a cup of Arabic coffee and a piece of baklava by Ahmad, the owner of the store. Ahmad and his family had immigrated from Beirut two years before Omar. By the time we left the store, we had an Arabic coffee set and enough Lebanese food to keep him happy until our next visit.

Memories up in Smoke

ONE WEEKEND MY parents were out of town for a few days and want to organize some of my things I had packed away before I had left for Paris. One of the boxes contained all the autographed Playbills from my years at the Mechanic Theatre.

Another box contained all my poems diaries from Cathy and pictures from my childhood and all the years that had followed, including photos of my family, friends, trips I had taken and pictures of different events in my life. There were a few mementoes I had kept over the years.

As I was going through some pictures, Omar came into the room. I was looking at a picture that was taken at a mother/daughter banquet when I had modeled Mrs. Robinsons' wedding gown. The theme of the banquet was wedding gowns of past and present.

My mother could not afford a wedding gown when my parents were married. Mrs. Robinson's daughter was too young to model it. Mrs Robinson was a friend of my mother and she and I were both about the same size, the gown was a perfect fit.

Omar looked at the picture of me wearing the gown and asked if I had been married before. "Oh no," I had said laughing. "This is just a picture I took modeling another woman's gown for a banquet I went to with my mom." Omar became angry and grabbed the photo from my hand. He thought I was lying to him and I tried telling him that I was never married before. He was aware of that and I didn't understand his doubting me.

Omar began gathering up all the boxes and took them downstairs. I followed him and he put them down before the fireplace. Before I realized what he was doing he lit a fire and began burning my pictures. I tried to stop him and he just pushed me away.

He continued to burn everything, my Playbills my poems and diaries. I was shocked and very upset. How could he be doing this? Why did he think he had the right to burn things that obviously meant something to me?

I saw a side of Omar that I didn't want to see and it scared me. I left the room to compose myself, and fortunately he left me alone. Nothing could change what he had done and the last thing I wanted to do was to make him angry. So, I said nothing. The incident was never brought up again.

Rob's Birth

I WAS THREE weeks past my due date so I had an appointment to go to the hospital to hopefully, induce labor. I was given the drug Patosin and it looked as if I would go into labor. After a few hours, my contractions stopped. The doctor assured me that the baby was fine.

Disappointed, I went home and rested. Later that evening my waters broke. Until the contractions got closer all I could do was wait. My mom and Omar played cards until it was time to go to the hospital.

After signing into the hospital, I was taken up to my room and hooked up to the monitors to measure my contractions. Eighteen hours and two doctors later, the next doctor on duty started her shift. My doctor asked if I would like some medication for the pain. I was so exhausted I said "yes".

Omar was furious that I wouldn't deliver without medication. He began shouting at me and the doctor. Omar was making so much noise that security was called and came into the labor room. Omar was told to leave and when he refused, he was escorted out of the maternity ward. My mom was in the waiting room and came in to be with me and calm me down.

I began getting sick and was weak because of it. Since the baby hadn't begun to move down the birth canal, my doctor told me it would have to be a "C" section. As the doctor left the room to prep for surgery, the baby began to move. I was quickly wheeled into the delivery room and my baby was born.

He was the most beautiful baby I had ever seen. My son looked around with his big brown eyes and a full head of hair. My dad had come right from work so both of my parents were admiring their first grandchild.

When Omar calmed down and cooled off he was allowed to come in and see his son. Although I was embarrassed by Omar, I wouldn't let him ruin this moment for me.

A Place of Our Own

WHEN ROB WAS three months old Omar's English had improved, his job was secure and we had saved enough money to get our own apartment. Omar had bought a used car so we could get around. We found a place not far from my parents. I felt as if we had finally settled down. Since I had my own apartment before I married Omar, we didn't need much to start out.

On weekends we often went to yard sales with my brother Dave and his wife Debbie and picked up some things we needed for the apartment. My mom would babysit, giving us time to have a couple of hours for lunch and to hang out with Dave.

Dave had a very calming effect on Omar. When Omar was relaxed he could be a lot of fun and was good company. I wished it happened more often.

Occasionally Omar and I had guests over for dinner and he would cook the meal. He had several dished that were his specialty. Omar enjoyed cooking and entertaining both family and friends.

Omar was charming, loving and funny when he was happy, but when he was worried or frustrated, he was a totally different person. Omar was like Dr. Jeckel and Mr. Hyde. I was never sure what caused him to be Dr. Jeckel.

For a while, I worked with Omar at the factory. He was in the sewing area and I worked on the assembly line, fusing pieces together, but we saw reach other at smoke breaks and lunch.

Standing on my feet all day, taking care of Rob, and keeping up with the house proved to be too much for me. My ankles were swollen and my legs hurt when I finished work. My doctor told me to quit. I needed a job where I wasn't standing all day. Even though the extra money helped we decided I would wait until Rob was a bit older to get a job. If I was to go back to work, I wanted to work for my dad and go back to dental assisting. But, Omar preferred that I stayed home and take care of Rob and the house. I loved being home with Rob.

Keeping up with the wash was part of taking care of the house and Omar expected it to be done when he came home. Washing machines and dryers were across the parking lot in a building of its own. That meant balancing the wash, while pushing Rob in his stroller.

One day, my next-door neighbor, Jack, was outside tinkering with a radio. Noticing me trying to balance the wash and the stroller, he offered to watch Rob while I went to the laundry room to work on the wash. I was grateful for his offer. From that day on, Jack would watch Rob for me while I did the laundry.

Between the wash and dry cycles, we would talk about things in general. Jack was retired and lived with his daughter, Cindy and her son, Jim. Jack was almost always outside and usually tinkering with some appliance, either to fix it or see how it worked.

Eventually I opened up to him and mentioned Omar's temper. He was aware of Omar's temper already Jack could hear him yelling through the walls. I was glad to get it off my chest that I was worried and sometimes scared of Omar. It was a big relief just knowing Jack was next door and aware that things could turn violent.

Chapter 5

Immigration of the Farahs

The Vision

Starting Immigration

Red Tape

Preparation for the Farahs

Shut the Door and Open a Window

The Arrival

A Dream comes true

Making a New Life in America

Trouble in the Family

The Vision

AFTER OMAR WENT to work in the morning, I would watch
Good Morning America. During the news one morning, there
was a segment on Beirut. Some of the news footage showed some Lebanese
civilians, running down the street screaming, running for their lives and
dodging gunfire.

As I watched, I saw Omar's aunt Suad, running among the fearful crowd.
Adnon, Suad's brother and Omar's youngest uncle, was also in the frantic
crowd. I could hardly believe what I was seeing.

During my time in Beirut, I had spent a lot of time with both of them as
their apartment was very close to the Farahs. I had spent a lot of time with
Suad just drinking tea and chatting. I met Suad on my first day in Beirut.
Since Suad spoke English, she started teaching me Lebanese and also the
Lebanese customs.

I was very fond of both her and Adnon. And now, here she was, running
for her life on the news. I became very upset and prayed for the safety of
them and other people I cared about. I began thinking about the Farahs
and wondered what would become of them. Very soon after thinking about
them I had a vision.

Omar, Rob and I were at the airport. Other people, family and friends, were waiting with us. The plane landed and among the people arriving were Omar's parents, Maroon and Ahlena, with Nadia holding her newborn daughter Karen. Pierre, Simon and Sarah followed them in a crowd of people on the same plane.

Omar and I greeted them with hugs kisses and tears. Mrs. Farah reached over to take Rob from my arms as she went on to cuddle and kiss her grandson. In turn, Omar and I were greeting them. Then the vision ended.

For the rest of the morning, I thought about the vision, wondering if I could actually bring them here. Later that day I told Omar about the newscast and my vision.

After dinner we watched the news and the same broadcast of Beirut was shown. Omar was upset to see his aunt running in terror from the gunfire. The street was not far from his parents house and he was very worried about them.

I again mentioned the vision and the fact that it had put an idea in my head to bring them here. If it was possible to bring his family to the States, would they leave Lebanon?

Omar was worried about them living in Beirut, but, considering his parents age and his mothers cancer, he wasn't sure if they would consider leaving Lebanon. With the conditions in Beirut, it was a dangerous and difficult there with little promise of a secure future.

Starting Immigration

A FEW WEEKS after seeing the vision, Omar took his first vacation from work. We had been in the States for nearly a year and Omar had wanted to visit some friends in upstate New York.

His friends were neighbors and close friends of the Farahs when they lived in Beirut. It had been eight years since Omar had seen his friend, Ash and Omar was looking forward to the visit.

One evening, Omar, Ash and I were visiting at Ash's parents' house when news about Beirut came on the TV. News concerning the escalating fighting in Beirut was becoming an almost daily occurrence.

I made the comment that I wanted to bring Omar's family here to America. Ash's sister turned around and looked at me as she said, "Who are you?"

I said nothing but she continued, "Who do you know that you could bring the whole family here? Do you know someone important?"

She laughed at me as if I was a joke. I felt like a fool, and in one brief moment she had made me feel worthless. She looked at me from head to toe and continued laughing. Embarrassed, I left the room and never spoke another word to her.

Maybe I was nobody special, but whether someone laughed at me or not I was more determined than before to bring the Farahs to America. As I heard the news, I prayed, asking God to help me bring the family here.

After we returned from Plattsburgh, I called immigration and asked them what if anything I could do to bring the Farah's here. The lady at immigration gave me very little information and told me to call either my state senator or a Member of Congress. The senator's office was no help at all. So I called the office of Congresswoman Barbara Mikulski. Her office connected me to a man named Perry, who dealt with visa's and immigration Because the Farah's were not my blood relatives but Omar's, there was little I could do. Omar only had a green card. Perry was very understanding and said he would get back to me.

When Perry called me back he told me he had been doing some checking for me. The task would be difficult but not impossible. There would be a long and difficult road ahead.

Because Omar and I had very little money and with that many people, we would have to have a sponsor and a place for them to live. It would take the backing of a large organization or my church.

Perry told me about Lutheran Immigration and that they might be able to help me. They had helped many churches sponsor a family. The fact the my church is Lutheran would not change the outcome was, but it would not hurt. I called Lutheran Immigration if they could help me being the Farahs here.

Red Tape

WHEN I CALLED Lutheran Immigration I was told that since Omar was not a citizen, the Farah's would have to have a sponsor before they would even consider helping us.

They suggested I ask my church for help. If my church agreed to sponsor the Farahs, the church would have to agree to back the Farahs financially. Forms would have to be filled out by the church and approved by Lutheran Immigration. The church would then have to find a place for them to live and find jobs for the Farah's who could work. It would be a long process but our only chance to help the Farahs.

I called church to talk to my Pastor about the Farah's situation Lutheran Immigration and the possibility of sponsoring them. After discussing all the facts as I understood them, it was planned that I would talk to the church council during their monthly meeting in two weeks.

I was thrilled thinking we could do this. I thanked my pastor for listening and help.

Inside, I was excited and hopeful but then there was Omar. What should I say to him? Should I wait until something definite has been decided? Omar needed to know what was going on and be at the meeting with me.

Preparations for the Farahs

O N THE NIGHT of the Church Council meeting, Omar and I were both nervous and excited. Being able to bring the Farahs to America depended on the Council's decision. I wrote down what I needed to tell and ask the Church, along with what Perry had said we needed for support.

At the meeting I presented my request. While the Council talked it over, Omar and I paced outside the hall. It didn't take the Council long to make a decision, and it was a unanimous, "yes".

Omar and I were very excited and optimistic. The Church would organize a committee to get things started and I had to call Perry to find out how to proceed. The next thing I had to do was to convince the Farahs to leave Lebanon.

Before we started to work on Immigration, Omar called his family to see if they would come to the States if it was possible. There would be no point in starting Immigration if they didn't want to come here.

Telephone lines were working so Omar called his family to let them know what was going on. He told Maroon that my church had agreed to sponsor them and that papers had been sent to the U.S. Immigration to start the paperwork process.

Our chance of being approved was encouraging and Maroon was cautiously excited and would tell the family. We would call and keep them updated.

After the church council approved the sponsoring of the Farahs, a committee would be formed to get things organized for their arrival. One of the council members owned several row houses that he rented out. He generously offered one of his houses for the Farahs, for one year, rent-free. The house just needed a little touching up with paint and general cleaning, for the new tenants.

During the next Sunday church service, the president of the church council told the congregation about their decision to sponsor the Farahs.

Committees needed to be formed to help with the different needs of the family. The church was buzzing with excitement and volunteers for committees were quickly organized.

A subcommittee was appointed that just dealt with finding jobs for five of the Farahs who could work. Age and the language barrier was an issue to be considered. Mr. Farah was in his 60's and spoke no English. Maroon was fluent in English with medical training while Simon and Pierre, teenagers spoke some English but were working hard on improving it.

Mrs. Farah had cancer, but she was able to watch Maroon and Nadias little girls while they worked.

Sarah needed to finish her education and was helping her mom take care of herself and the girls after school.

Since we knew where the house was located, I went to the school in her district and talked to admissions about her classes and her enrollment. A bus would pick her up on the corner from her house.

During the day, I would keep in touch with Perry. Since the paper work was now with the US Embassy, Perry could keep track of how things were progressing.

Weekend were full of working on getting the house ready. As furniture and household items became available, we would set them up in the house. Maroon had given me sizes for the family and when clothes were donated, Omar and I would sort through them.

The generosity of people was amazing. Even non-members, who had heard about the Farahs, donated things. Everything was coming together.

The church had a Christmas tree sale, along with bake sales and a dinner with all proceeds going to the Farah's to help them get settled when they arrived.

Aside from the fact that people were helping strangers, they were working and meeting with other members and people that they had only previously seen. Many new friendships were formed.

I was so thankful and proud of the work and time that so many people put into the preparation. The only question was when would they arrive?

Shut the Door and Open a Window

AFTER ALL THE work the church had done to help get ready for the Farahs, I was told the immigration quota for Lebanese allowed in the country was filled. Nothing short of a miracle would change that. I was devastated.

First I had to get the Farah's on the list. Perry had no idea of what to do or how to do it. I needed to get the attention of someone important who could help me with getting the Farah's added to the list. I thought of the idea of sending a telegram to the White House and somehow get someone's attention.

After months of almost daily persistence and hundreds of dollars in phone bills, not to mention my time, I could barely believe what I was hearing. When I told Omar, he was furious with me; I had built up both his family and his hope, only to let them down.

A few days later Perry called. There was a special quota plan be submitted to the House of Representatives for approval. If the plan was approved, 90 Lebanese refugees would be allowed to come to the States. But, they must be refugees. To be refugees they would have to leave Lebanon and go to Cyprus or Greece.

Not knowing what else to do about getting the Farahs on the list, I did send a telegram to the White House. Fortunately, the telegram got in the hands of the then Attorney General, Griffin Bell. In the telegram, I had begged for help with my plight.

Not long afterwards, I received news that the Farahs had been added to the list. My biggest problem now, was to get in touch with the Farahs and talk them into leaving Lebanon as refugees.

Omar worked during the day and it was hard for him to contact his family after work. Because of the time difference, it would be dark in Beirut when Omar arrived home from work.

Because of the heavy fighting, the Farahs, friends and neighbors lived in the basement shelter where no lights would be seen at night. It also made it impossible for them to hear the phone if we had tried to call. There was only a small window of time to call Beirut during the day.

When I tried to call Farahs, the operator told me all lines to Beirut were down. Contacting anyone in Beirut was difficult because of such problems. I was very persistent and tried to call at least once a day. One particular day, I got a very compassionate operator. I told her how important it was that I get through to them, if at all possible. The lines to Beirut were open that day, but she was not getting through to the Farahs' number.

I asked her to please try again. This time the operator got through to the Farahs' number, but no one answered the phone. I asked her to let it ring for a while.

As she let it ring, I explained to her that since they were living in the shelter under their building, if they did hear the phone, it would take them a while to get to it. So, she let it ring for a long time. Finally, my mother-in-law answered the phone.

The funny thing was that my mother-in-law had never heard the phone until she reached her apartment. Our timing had been perfect. The phone hadn't been working for several days. She had come upstairs to get something she needed.

With what Lebanese I knew, I did my best to tell her that for them to be able to come to the US, they would have to leave Lebanon and go to the American Embassy in either Cyprus or Greece. I told them that I believed it was God's will. Everything and everyone would be okay.

Luckily, Maroon had come up to see why his mother was taking so long and she put him on the phone. I explained everything to Maroon about how they must be refugees to be able to come to the States.

I told Maroon about the quota being filled and the special list that had been added and that they were all on the list. But to stay on the list, they must be refugees.

Maroon was also concerned about leaving everything they had at Lebanon and going to Cyprus only to find out they wouldn't be allowed to come to the States. I told him, he had to trust me.

Maroon was worried about having enough money to go to Cyprus. The Farahs sold their apartment and anything else they could and left the rest.

Maroon had some good news for me; his wife Nadia had had their baby, a little girl and they were both doing fine. They had named her Karen, after me.I was touched and told him so. With a lump in my throat, I sent my love and congratulations. I prayed for their swift and safe arrival in Cyprus.

The Arrival

M Y PARENTS-IN-LAW, MAROON and Nadia sold their apartments and any possessions they could sell for money to get to Cyprus.

They carried what they could and left the rest. They went up the coast from Beirut and took a boat to Cyprus.

When the Farahs arrived in Cyprus, they met other Lebanese at the embassy. Some people had been there for months, while others had been there for over a year trying to get to America.

After seeing all the people who were waiting to come to America, Maroon nervously talked to one of the immigration officers. Unfamiliar with the Farahs situation and the special immigration lists, the immigration officer said, "NO", they could not go to the United States.

Nervous and upset, Maroon called me early in the morning and said that the immigration officer wanted to talk to me.

Even though Maroon had told them about our government's approval, immigration needed confirmation. The immigration officer spoke very little English, and I spoke no Greek. I told the officer, I would have Perry call him as soon as Perry came to work.

Maroon got back on the line I told him not to panic and to stay put. Even though they were denied their visa to the States, I told Maroon I would take care of it.

It would be another hour, at least before Perry would be in his office. All I could do as the time slowly ticked away was to pace the floor and pray.

Finally, the hour had passed and I called Perry. I told him what was happening and he told me not to worry, all the papers were in order. Since Perry spoke fluent Greek he had no problem talking to the immigration officer.

Perry called me back and told me everything was straightened out and that the Farahs would fly into Baltimore and would arrive that evening. After all the months of preparations, I couldn't believe it was finally happening.

The news media heard about the story and wanted to do a story for the TV news. Omar had at first said no. He was worried about people knowing too much about them. He did agree to let the newspaper do an article about his family but to omit the fact that they were Christian and where they would live. They agreed and were at the airport when we arrived.

Omar and I got to the airport early. Rob, my parents and a few friends were there to greet them. Their plane arrived on time.

The passengers began to come down the ramp. There they were, all nine of them, looking tired and nervous, but happy. It was a moment that anyone present, could not forget.

There were no dry eyes in the crowd. We ran to greet them with hugs and kisses. There was so much excitement between the hellos and introductions, I almost didn't believe it was real; the whole scenario was just like my vision. I might have been an instrument in bringing them here, but I could certainly not have done it alone.

As my mother-in-law turned again to hug her son and hold her grandson, I got to hold my namesake, Karen.

I thought about the voice I had heard in Paris and about the faith, love and determination; everything that made this all possible.

A Dream Come True

AFTER GATHERING UP the small amount of baggage the Farahs brought with them, we all headed to the cars to take them to their house. The Farahs knew they had a place to stay, but had no idea it was a fully furnished house with clothes in the closet and food in the cupboards.

When we arrived at their house, the porch light was on and someone had left one on in the front room. The Farahs could not believe that the house was for them to live in. The shock continued as they entered the front room.

Flowers and a large basket of fruit were on the table. Someone had filled the refrigerator with all the staples they would need for a few days. For them it was like walking into a model home. They could barely believe what they were seeing. The most touching fact was that so many people had worked together to furnish a house for them.

For several days people were coming and going through their front door. Some people brought food while others stopped by to welcome them to America. The Farahs could not believe the generosity and friendliness they were given. It was truly a rag to riches scenario.

After settling in their new home, the Farahs were all present at church the next Sunday. The Farah's stood before the congregation and were introduced. Maroon thanked the church for sponsoring them and helping me bring them to America. He also thanked them for the house, the furnishings, food and all the support they had received.

A reception in our church hall followed the service where the congregation and the Farahs were able to meet and talk to one another. Maroon, Omar and I did our best to translate conversations. I was pleased the reception was so well attended.

The following week, his family and I went to a meeting where Congresswoman Barbara Mikulski would be speaking. After standing in line to greet her our turn arrived and I introduced the Farahs to her. Maroon thanked her for her support with the immigration.

Perry, who had been so helpful and supportive throughout the whole course of immigration was present. He was excited to meet the Farahs. If it hadn't been for Perry's help, I would never have succeeded in bringing the Farah's here.

I thanked Perry for all his help and the extra time he had put in to the immigration. Including his patience and advice along the way. I told the Farahs that it was Perry who had called Cyprus and cleared the way for their departure to America.

I stepped back as they all thanked and hugged him. Faith and hope and the help of someone like Perry who believed in me, can sometimes move mountains.

Making a New Life in America

THE FARAHS HAD a month after arriving before they were to start their jobs. In that month, they could settle in, become familiar with the city and surrounding area.

We had to figure out transportation. The Farahs lived close to two main arteries, both of them on the bus routes.

The Farahs needed to work on their English and began to attend Mrs. Prodey's classes. Aside from her weekly classes, she began to come over to the Farah's house and tutored them once a week.

Mrs. Prodey and the Farah's got along well along well and they enjoyed each other company. She was interested in learning about their culture and was fond of Lebanese food. So it was lessons for a meal.

Mrs. Prodey became part of the family. She had us over for dinner one evening for a good American meal. Ham, turkey and the works. She enjoyed wine with her meals and shared a wine she had saved for a special occasion and it was. Mrs. Prodey was very Irish and loved to tell stories of her travels But she was also interested in other peoples experiences.

After dinner we sat outside in her backyard on her patio enjoying the evening and chatting. Mrs. Prodey got great satisfaction in hearing how their English was improving.

Within months after arriving, the Farahs had adjusted quickly to life in the States. The Farahs were doing well with their jobs and had become familiar enough with Baltimore that they could get around the city on their own.

They eventually saved enough money between themselves to buy a used car, giving them some independence. With two cars between us, we were able to drive to a park for a cookout or spend time fishing, their favorite pastime.

When Robert would fly in from Paris, it was like a holiday; he brought gifts for everyone. On the day he arrived, there would be a feast and celebration. Sometimes he would bring a cousin or an uncle with him to visit the family.

Robert loved the nightlife and Omar and I would go with him to a club and go dancing for an evening. Maroon and Nadia would join us and we enjoyed getting together in a relaxed environment.

Robert was surprised and pleased that everything had gone so well with his family's settling in and with how much so many people had given them and helped them get started.

It was always sad to see Robert leave He brought so much happiness with him, but at the same time we were grateful he was able to come over.

Maroon and Nadia worked hard saving money for a place of their own. When overtime was available, Maroon worked the extra hours. Several months before their first year in America, they were able to rent an apartment close to everyone.

Maroon and Nadia were happy in the States and Nadia was doing well with her English. Ahlena was picking up English which would make things easier when she started school in the fall.

I enjoyed spending time with Maroon, Nadia and the girls, so I was happy to visit with them. We got together on weekends and had each other over for dinner. When we had the chance we would have a special day when we visited parts of Baltimore.

Trouble in the Family

IT BECAME OBVIOUS to everyone that Omar's temper was out of control. Mrs. Farah, Maroon and Nadia had noticed a few of my bruises and began noticing a change in me. Nadia asked me if everything was ok with Omar. Was he hurting me?

I told her he was becoming physical, Omar had started pushing, kicking and hitting me. They gave each other a knowing but concerned look. Later I asked Nadia how the Farahs could take Omar's actions so lightly. Abuse wasn't a stranger to the family. Mrs. Farah was an abused wife. Nadia thankfully, was not.

One Sunday as Omar and I were visiting for dinner, Omar's father started yelling at his wife. He began to smack her around and hit her. The children were quickly taken outside by Sarah as both Omar and Maroon tried to hold their father back away from their mother.

Nadia and I went over to Mrs. Farah to make sure she was ok. She was shaken but unharmed. I could not believe what I had just witnessed, I had never seen a woman treated like that before.

During the fighting, the light fixture on the dining room ceiling was broken as well as a few other items in the house. Because of the yelling and screaming, I was afraid one of the neighbors had heard what was going on.

I was afraid someone from church would find out and want them out of the house.

After peace was finally restored, I just wanted to get Rob and go back to our apartment. I did not want to become involved in any fighting in the family.

I worried about Omar' temper. Am I next? Before we had left, Maroon told me he would talk to Omar and assured me that he and Nadia were there if I needed them.

Chapter 6

Shattered Dreams

Robs First birthday

Of Things to Come

Cindy

The Calm Before the Storm

The Final Straw

The Aftermath

A Common Bond

Visitation

Salt in the Wound

Emotional Healing

A Matter of Separation

Rob's First Birthday

WHEN ROB WAS a year old, I wanted to have a little party for him and invite some friends with children his age. I had asked Omar about it, but he said no, we would celebrate Rob's birthday with his family. I was disappointed because I rarely had the chance to visit with my friends anymore. Besides, it would be good for Rob to play with other children as well as Ahlena and Karen.

I had been thinking about this for several weeks before his birthday. Omar didn't want me to have people coming over when he wasn't there, except for family. Rob was too young to appreciate a party but I felt cheated by not being able to have friends over. I thought if it were just a few people coming over, Omar might change his mind.

That morning Omar called me from work, I told him I would like to have a small get together and told him who I'd like to have over. Instead of letting me go ahead, he said no and he was coming home from work to make sure I didn't have anyone over.

He sounded furious on the phone, so I called his brother Maroon and my mom, telling them what I did and about Omar coming home. I was scared and let my friends know not to come over.

Thankfully, when Omar came home, my mom and Maroon were already at our apartment. Omar began screaming like a mad man. I should have obeyed him, Omar yelled. But what about what I wanted?

It was just going to be a small get together. When he was about to grab me, Maroon held him back. It took awhile to calm him down enough for anyone to talk to him without an argument.

When Omar' temper had calmed down, my mom left being very upset with him. Omar, Rob and I left with Maroon to go to their parent's house. I blamed myself. If I had listened to Omar in the first place, nothing would have happened and all the upset would have been avoided.

Of Things to Come

BEFORE OMAR'S FAMILY had arrived, he was often moody and depressed. I blamed it on his worrying about his family in Lebanon as well as his adjusting to a new country. When we got our own apartment, Omar began treating me differently.

He slapped me around, pushed me down, yelled at me a lot and belittled me. Once he got annoyed with me and kicked me in the rear end. Gradually, the mental and physical abuse became worse. He resented me having any and little by little, I was losing part of myself, my self-respect and my identity.

When I had heard of a wife being beaten by her husband I had wondered what had happened or what she had done to be treated in such a way. I also wondered why a woman would stay and not leave her husband.

When it began happening to me, I learned firsthand. Fear. To beat you down physically, they must first beat you down emotionally. I felt humiliated. Part of the problem was my own pride and ignorance in the fact that I didn't want to admit to myself or anyone that Omar was becoming abusive. Except for the one time in Paris, he had never hit me.

One evening, he was in a very bad mood. He was late, stopping by his parents first after work. Dinner was cold. He began yelling at me first and then shoved me around.

I told him I wasn't going to tolerate his behavior anymore. I picked up the phone to have my brother pick Rob and me up, when he pulled the whole phone off the wall and threw it down on the kitchen floor.

"Who are you calling?" he screamed.

"Dave, I am not staying here the way you are acting!" I said angrily.

He grabbed a long butcher knife from the drawer and held it up to my throat telling me that if I left him, he would kill me.

There was always the fear of what was coming next. I had been to a lawyer. But, my visit didn't make me feel any better about my situation. To file for abuse, I would have to be hit and have obvious signs of abuse. Throwing things, yelling and threats could not be proven.

One night, Rob had been colicky and cried a lot, which got on Omar's nerves. Rob was only three months old. I tried my best to quiet him but with no success. I put him in his crib to get a bottle of juice for him and to put some Tylenol in the juice.

When I came back into the room, Omar had taken off his belt and repeatedly hit Rob with it. I went crazy and tried to pull the belt from his hands. Omar pushed me away.

"Oh God", I prayed. "Help my baby!" The harder I tried to stop him, the rougher he was with me. He threw me against the wall. He quit hitting Rob and left the room. Rob's little body was covered with welts and marks from the belt.

As gently as I could, I picked Rob up from the crib to hold him. I locked the door to the room, but I had no phone to call anyone. No real way to get out and avoid Omar. Eventually, Rob was asleep in his crib and I on the floor.

The next morning Omar knocked on the door, and I went over to look at his son. Rob was very swollen and serious bruises were appearing. I blamed myself and cried when Omar left the room. I took Rob from the crib and held him. A little later Omar wanted to come in. He wanted us to go to his parent's house.

As he glanced at Rob, he said "I'll kill you if you ever tell anyone what happened. If anyone asks he fell off a chair", he continued angrily.

My mother-in-law took one look at her grandson and gasped. She demanded to know what happened. I told her that he had fallen off a chair, as Omar looked on.

"This is not from falling off a chair. What happened?" She asked sternly.

I began to cry and told her what Omar had done. Omar looked at me like he was wanted to kill me. His mother immediately confronted her son but Omar insisted the welts and bruises came from falling. My mother-in-law said she knew better. The family was furious with Omar.

I was scared to leave and scared to stay. I vowed Rob would never be hurt again. It was only a short time until Rob and I would leave Omar.

Cindy

SINCE OMAR HAD ripped the phone out of the wall I had no way of contacting anyone. I had to let my parents and Dave know that my phone wasn't working. I went next door to ask if I can use the phone.

I was expecting Jack to open a door but it was his daughter, Cindy. Even though I barely knew her, I was glad she was there. Cindy opened the door and invited Rob and me in. I explained that my phone wasn't working she told me to use her phone. Thanking her, she offered me a cup of tea or coffee.

"I'd love a cup of tea, if this is a good time to you", I gladly replied.

She gently offered to take a Rob from me so I could use the phone. As she held Rob I called Dave and briefly let him know what had happened. After making sure I was okay he said he would come over after his class (at college). Until I was drinking my tea, I hadn't realized how much my hands were shaking.

"Are you okay?" she calmly asked, "I heard a lot of shouting and noise last night. My dad mentioned you were having problems with your husband" she continued. "And if I can help in any way . . ."

Before she could finish, I lost it. All the dirty, little secrets, of me falling and bumping into the things, the fear, the denial, the slapping around and kicking me, making me so submissive that it allowed him to overpower me and sodomize me. Sodomy was his way of punishment; his pleasure and my pain and humility. I hated him for it.

When I went to a lawyer even he made me feel as if all that wasn't enough for me to charge Omar with anything. I had no proof of my abuse. I was told by my lawyer, that until he hit me again, I had nothing to help me in my defense.

Cindy shook her head and seemed so sympathetic. I was surprised that I told her so much, but her eyes and expression told me she understood my pain. I was crying and shaking. On one hand, it felt good to be able to confide in another woman about it, on the other hand, I felt bad for unloading all this on Cindy, whom I had only met briefly on two other occasions.

We sat there in silence for a while until Cindy said; "if he hits you or threatens you again come over or bang on the wall."

"Thanks," I mumbled, "or call 911 for me."

"How did you know?" I asked. "What made you think I was being abused other than the noise and what your father had said?"

"Whenever you are walking with him, to or from your house, you walk behind him with your head down. And, you have gotten so thin, almost anorexic."

"You are observant", I replied.

"I have seen it in other women before", she stated.

I looked at her and shook my head, knowingly.

"I better go and get some work done before he gets home, thanks for listening and the use of your phone", I replied still shaking, but calmer, then I was.

"Will you be all right when he comes home?" She asked.

"My brother is coming over, he is aware of what is going on, but thanks."

"Take care of yourself, someone is usually always here. I get home by 5:00, but today I had taken the day off. My dad is always here", she said.

Thanking her again, I picked up Rob and asked if we could talk again soon.

"Any time I am home", she replied, smiling.

Cindy was good to her word. She began to say hello when Omar, Rob and I went to the car. We began to get together and talk. Little did I know then, that Cindy would become one of the best friends I would ever have.

The Calm Before the Storm

DAVE CAME OVER that afternoon before Omar was home from work. Dave stayed until he was sure Omar had calmed down from the night before. Dave and I were very close and he and Debbie were over often so Omar didn't think anything of Dave being at our apartment when he came home. Omar liked Dave which also helped. Dave began coming over every morning to check on Rob and me, to make sure we were okay.

Omar's boss asked if he was willing to work overtime on Saturdays and Omar said yes. He was home by two so it wasn't as long a day. The money helped out and I began getting together with Cindy for several hours on Saturdays.

Cindy and I had a lot of common interests, hobbies and music and we were becoming close friends. At least twice, aside from Saturdays, Cindy and I got together with her friend Carol and I began going to ceramic classes with them.

I was pleasantly surprised at Omar letting me go. After class, we usually went out for coffee and tea. I enjoyed my evenings out with Cindy and Carol. I could relax and they were both very supportive.

For about two months, Omar was a lot calmer and I began to feel more positive about our marriage. There were still the days when I felt as if I was walking on eggshells, but it was not as often.

Dave and Debbie were very excited about becoming parents and when their son was born Omar and I went to the hospital to see the baby. Omar was very upbeat that night and I was happier than I had been in a long time.

The Final Straw

I KNEW IT was going to be a bad night when he walked through the door. It was late and Omar had eaten dinner with his parents and he was in a bad mood. The best thing to do was to stay out of his way.

I worried about every little thing I did in order to keep harmony between us. There was no keeping him happy that evening. One thing led to another and we began to have an argument. I was glad our baby was asleep in his crib.

How can this be going on? Only the night before Omar had been so pleasant and relaxed. We had gone to see Dave and Debbie's baby. Omar had sat in the room chatting and being charming. When we came back from the hospital, Omar was kind and affectionate. He was the man I had fallen in love with.

I remember thinking we could make this marriage work. I thought about those people who had told me to leave Omar. How could I leave the father of my child who could be such a happy, kind and affectionate man? But then there was this other side to Omar.

Omar began pushing me around and yelling at me. He slapped me hard across my left cheek and I put my hand on my face to gently rub my cheek to ease the pain. The worst thing I could do was to fight back, so I turned to go to bed when WHAM! He hit me hard down the back of my head with a heavy alarm clock. WHAM! he hit me again and this time I saw stars and colors before my eyes. WHAM!

After this final blow I felt as if I was going to faint but he grabbed me by my hair. He pushed me on the floor as he tried to bang my head on the bare floor. Fortunately, by instinct, I held my hands up over my head.

"Oh God! Please don't let me die! My baby is in the next room. Who will protect him? Please make him stop!"

At that point, he let go of my hair and began kicking me as I lay in a fetal position. He rolled me over several times with his foot and continued to kick and scream at me like a maniac.

"Get up and get out of here before I kill you", he screamed as he followed me down the hall to our bedroom. I was dizzy and in such pain that I could hardly walk.

When we passed Rob's bedroom, I wanted to stay in the room with him. Omar would not let me see him and I was too scared to risk making him angrier. With my hands raw and bloody from the pounding, I crawled into bed. Omar turned out the light before he left the room.

As I lay in bed shaking with fear I listened for any sound of him bothering Rob. I prayed Omar would fall asleep and thanked God I was alive. I cried into my pillow to muffle the sound. After what seemed like hours I finally drifted off to sleep.

The next morning Omar came in our bedroom to wake me up for work. He never said a word about the night before.

Stay calm, get the baby dressed The sooner I can get myself ready and get to my parents' house, the better.

I was in such pain that it was difficult to get ready. I was very scared of Omar and felt as if I was on autopilot.

Don't cry, don't talk, and don't do anything to aggravate him, I thought.

I was thankful it was my mom's Saturday to watch Rob. As soon as Omar dropped us off at my parents, I locked the door and watched for him to drive away. When he was out of sight, I cried as I told my parents what had happened.

Within minutes I was off to see my family doctor to make sure I was okay and also to have the doctor make a record of my injuries. The doctor took care of the cuts on my hands and knuckles as he bandaged them up. The three knots on my head were the size of golf balls. But luckily, except for a few bruises and brush burns, nothing was broken.

I was then taken to a friend of the family's house where I would be safe and could call the police. My brother, his wife and their three day old son were at home with my mom and Rob. They would make sure that Omar could not get in the house to harm anyone.

After talking to the police on the phone, I felt a little safer knowing that they were on their way over to talk to me and make a report. While I waited, our friends did their best to console me and to try to calm me down.

My head was hurting so much I could hardly think straight and my body still shook with fear. I could barely hold my cup of tea with two hands without spilling it. When the two policemen arrived, I began to tell them what happened. My hands were obvious but I wanted them to feel the bumps on my head.

"Is he home now?" One of the policemen asked. "No", I said knowing that he was going to his parent's house. "Are you sure?" He asked.

"Yes but I can call my girlfriend who lives next door and ask her to check for me."

The policemen thought it would be a good idea to call, and I briefly told her what was going on.

"If you can get someone to help you get some things out of your apartment, we will go with you to make sure he doesn't bother you if he comes home", the one officer said.

My two other brothers were at work. But, after picking up Debbie and their newborn son from the hospital, Dave got two of his friends to help him move me out of the apartment. We met the two policemen at my apartment. My girlfriend Cindy, and her dad helped us as we got what Rob and I needed, plus a few things that were mine and were special to me.

We filled up the car planning to come back for another load, but when we came back, Omar was there. He was screaming at the police telling them I was lying. The one policeman told Omar to calm down but Omar continued yelling at us and calling me a liar.

"He's crazy" the other policeman said. "You can't even talk to him."

"I know" I said, suddenly embarrassed that he was my husband. It was agreed that Omar could take what he needed and I could come back for anything else, since almost everything we owned had been mine anyway. But when we came back later, almost everything had been taken. He had wiped me out.

In the middle of our empty living room was our once decorated Christmas tree, standing bare, after all the lights and ornaments had been taken off.

"Mommy, look at my tree!" Rob cried.

My heart ached for him and I wished Omar had just taken the whole thing.

Omar was given a restraining order to leave Rob and me alone. When my other two brothers found out about what Omar had done, they were ready to practically kill him, but the police warned that my brothers could be arrested for assault.

I did not press charges against Omar because it would have meant Omar would lose his green card and his family would be sent back to Beirut. I did not want that to happen.

The Aftermath

AFTER REPEATEDLY TRYING to call me at my parents' house with no success, Omar called Dave and said how sorry he was for what he had done. All he wanted to do was at least talk to me. If I agreed, we would meet at his parents' house where I knew he would not hurt me.

Dave was the peacemaker in the family and he agreed to talk to Omar. Dave came over to our parents' house and talked to me. He did not want me to go back with Omar but to see if we could at least talk and calm him down a bit. Against my better judgment and my parents' disapproval, I agreed to talk to Omar if Dave was with me. Leaving Rob with my parents, Dave and I went to the Farahs to talk to Omar.

When we arrived, the family hugged and kissed me as if nothing had happened. One look at me said it all and Nadia began to cry as the others glared at Omar with astonished disapproval. Everyone said how Omar should never have treated me like he did and assured me it would never happen again. They insisted that Omar loved me.

From the time I arrived and throughout my entire visit, all I could do was cry. How did my marriage get so bad? Mrs. Farah kept trying to get me to calm down and stop crying. She told me it was not good for me to cry so much.

Crying wasn't good for me? What about what her son had done to me and Rob? What was wrong with me? I had barely escaped with my life and my son and here they were talking about our getting back together. Before I had gone over to the Farahs, I had to take medicine for the pain and a strong sedative.

More than anything I had wanted my marriage to work and would have done almost anything to make it work; but not this. I looked around the house and most of my furniture and other things were in boxes. Very few of the other things were what we had bought together.

Anger and fear began to creep up in me and I started to shake uncontrollably. All I wanted to do was get out of there and get back to my baby. I told Omar that I was too upset to talk about it anymore. I was shaking so hard at this point that Dave got me out of there.

Between the pain and sedatives the doctor had given me, I was in and out of consciousness for two days. Once, I woke up screaming after a bad dream about Omar, Phil ran in the room and assured me that I was safe. Safe. What a beautiful word.

With Omar there was always the fear of what was coming next. Even when I was dealing with the present horror of what was happening when he beat me and how I might stop it; I had hoped it would change.

I waited for an apology that never came. All I got was denial that anything ever happened. This time was too serious to deny or live with it any longer.

It was time to accept the truth that the violence would not end and I had to walk away now and go on with my life without Omar.

A Common Bond

O N MONDAY I got dressed and ready for work like any other morning, except it wasn't just like any other morning. I had had a traumatic weekend and my life had turned upside down. Rob stayed with my mom because I was scared to let him out of my sight, and I felt safer knowing he was at my parent's house.

Even though I was still very nervous and in pain; I felt the sooner I returned to a normal routine, the better. Aside from the patients from a private practice, my dad also took care of the inmates at the Baltimore County Jail. The inmates were brought to our office usually by at least two policemen.

One of the policemen and I were talking about what had happened and he asked me why I had put up with it for so long. I told him that I had truly believed that marriage was "till death do us part."

He quickly asked, "Yeah, but whose death?" He was quick to point out that he had seen plenty of domestic violence, being a policeman, and that it only got worse, not better.

That evening, my oldest brother Phil took me for counseling at the House of Ruth; a shelter in Baltimore for battered women and children. It was group therapy and as I entered the room, I was surprised by how many women were there. There were at least 25 to 30 women of all ages and races in the group. Some of the women had physical signs of abuse while others had been emotionally beaten down and had "the look" that had occasionally stared back at me in the mirror.

The leader of the group introduced herself and began to tell us about the House of Ruth, mainly its facilities and counseling available to battered women. She then revealed to us that she too had been abused, afraid and ashamed to accept the fact that the man she had married and loved would beat her. She lost all her self-confidence, her pride, her zest for life, and along with that, she had lost part of herself.

She was clear that the most important thing that we had to accept and deal with was what had happened in our lives.

After she had finished talking, she had asked if anyone was willing to share a little about what had brought them here and share their story. Most of us were reluctant at first, but we all began sharing at least part of our lives and experiences. It was a relief to talk to others who understood what we were going through.

The women were from all walks of life. Young and old, rich and poor, a professional or a housewife; everyone had a story someone else could relate to. There were a lot of tears shed and many times someone would reach out and squeeze another woman's hand or give a hug.

Their pain was our pain. An unfortunate happening that brought us together. We shared our stories and our pain as we drew strength from one another. Somehow, we promised ourselves, we will get through all of this.

The men who abused these women were as diverse as the women. The lady sitting next to me said her husband was a good father, a successful businessman and a good neighbor, and went to church every Sunday with his family. But, there she was sitting next to me with a swollen face and a very puffy black and blue eye. She had tolerated it years because, in spite of the beatings, she believed he was a good man.

After several sessions of group therapy, I felt it was time to make it on my own. Realizing it wasn't entirely my fault, I knew I had to start believing in myself again.

Visitation

THE WEEK AFTER I had left Omar, I had an appointment with my lawyer to file for separation papers and sole custody of Rob. A few days after my visit to the lawyer, I was at work when I received papers from Omar's lawyer to appear before a judge; Omar was contesting my appeal for sole custody.

Ironically, Cindy and I had plans that evening to see the movie Kramer vs. Kramer that had just come to the theaters. The movie dealt with a man who fought for and won, sole custody of his son. Although the situation in the movie was unlike mine, I was too upset over Omar's request for custody to see the movie.

Even though I had the doctor's records to support the fact that Omar was abusive, I was both scared and worried to think I could possibly lose sole custody or that Omar could be granted joint custody. As it turned out, Omar was granted visitation rights one evening a week for a few hours and one day every other weekend with no overnight visitation.

The first time Omar was granted visitation for a day was on Christmas. It broke my heart that I would miss out on celebrating Christmas with Rob and my family. My parents were going to my brother's house for a family dinner Not wanting to see Omar, they left early in the day. I spent the day alone. It was not until Rob was back that I could relax and enjoy what was left of the day.

Omar wanted more time with Rob. I could understand him wanting to see more of his son. But I was worried about any possible abuse to Rob or that he wouldn't bring him back. My documented injuries and the reports of Omar being abusive to both Rob and me, did little to prevent overnight visitations.

Omar managed to get a court order allowing him two overnight visitations a month on the weekend and one evening a week. During Rob's first overnight visit, I was very anxious and worried but, Omar had moved in with his parents. I felt better knowing Omar would not be alone with Rob.

Rob was too young to understand his parents separation, so visitation became a normal routine. Rob spent time with his grandparents, aunts, uncles and cousins, all who loved him. He was well cared for when he was with Omar. Rob was content to spend time with his father and he was a happy little boy.

As time went on, I became more relaxed when he was with Omar. I began to look at the visitation as a break, a time for myself. But, I was always happy and relieved to have Rob back home with me.

Salt in the Wound

THE BRUISES AND cuts on my hands had pretty much healed, but the three bumps on my head were still there, although considerably smaller. The pain caused from being hit still came like sharp surges of pain, in my head. My doctor said the pain was caused by the healing of nerve endings caused by the blows to my head.

He told me it could take months before the pain was gone. I could understand and deal with the pain knowing it would eventually go away. But I had to deal with other pain that would take longer to heal, and even longer to accept.

Not long after I left Omar, I had a long talk with my Pastor which was supposed to be confidential. Assuming it was, I "bared my soul" when I spoke about my marriage. It wasn't long before I found out that my "private" conversation had become public knowledge.

On Sundays when I went to church, too many members would look at me and whisper to others around them. At first I thought I was just being paranoid, but a "true" friend of mine told me what was circulating throughout the church. I was shocked, disappointed and hurt.

The truth had torn my heart and sent stabbing pains in my stomach. I felt betrayed. To make it worse, the woman who had spread the story was the "friend" I went to see the day after I was badly beaten and the police came to her house. If that wasn't bad enough, people began to say that Omar married me just come to America.

Was I so worthless that Omar had not have loved me? The other story was that Omar used me to bring his family to America. Although I was upset by the pettiness of that rumor, bringing the Farahs to the States was all my idea.

My life was difficult enough for me at that time without having to know what fellow "Christians" were saying. My life had become an open book, causing me to feel humiliated.

I have lived with an inferiority complex my whole life; this only seemed to verify it. I had two choices, run from it or hold my head high and ignore the stares and comments. I chose the latter.

Some members complained openly that after all the work the church did to support them and help them start a new life, this was their thanks? My church had agreed to help nine refugees escape a war-torn country and start a new life in the land of the free and they did that.

The Farahs were very grateful for all the Church had done and were just as disappointed as I was that things worked out the way they did.

My mom used to say that "the devil works the hardest in church" and I had to agree with that.

Emotional Healing

ANGER IS TOTAL frustration in the worst way. All the mean, bad and ugly emotions you can come up with. Anger challenges you to change your situation or environment and move on to do something that does not put you in that frame of mind. It encourages you to react and keep walking away.

I was told that by experiencing anger I was actually taking a big step in my emotional healing. It's not that I was angry all the time Fortunately, I had too many responsibilities for that. I had a son to raise who didn't need an angry mom. Rob was too happy and loving to deserve that.

The mere suggestion from Omar to get together was thwarted by my anger of being treated like I had been. But, emotional pain was still there. Both Cindy and Carol were quick to remind me how my life had been and that relationship like mine, don't change if I were to go back to Omar.

Women who are abused were often abused emotionally and/or physically as children or teenagers. I was one of them. The last thing I wanted was to be hurt or treated badly. I often thought it was my inability to stand up for myself.

It is one thing to say "I must believe in myself" and another to actually do it. There is no magic potion The strength I needed must be in me. I had made it through difficult times before and I would make it through this.

A Matter of Separation

NOT LONG AFTER Omar and I separated, Omar's brother, Robert, flew in from Paris. While he was in Baltimore he had wanted to talk to me. Hoping to air a few things, I agreed. Robert told me that Omar and his family loved me and that no one wanted to see us divorce.

"I'm glad, but that doesn't change anything. Tell me, if your sister came home and told you that her husband would lose his temper and hit her, would you tell her to go back to him or to leave him?"

He looked at me but said nothing.

"That's what I thought" I said quietly, trying to stay calm. "Then why ask me to go back and take it?"

A few days later, I drove to my favorite spot in Pennsylvania. Alone, I walked down the path to the rock that overlooked the stream. I sat on the rock and looked around, listening to the trickling of the stream and the rustling of the leaves. I tried to imagine Jesus sitting next to me as a friend of mine would. Quietly, I began talking to Jesus, calling on Him to hear me.

"I know we must forgive, but what if someone denies they ever hurt us? The more I forgive, the worse it is the next time. I live in constant fear of him. What about my son? Isn't it my responsibility to protect him? Is this the kind of marriage you speak of? Forgive me, I know I made mistakes too, but I can't go back."

I watched the clear, sparkling water as it trickled over the rocks and stones in the stream. The wind gently blew through the trees as I leaned against the base of a big tree. I closed my eyes and began to feel an inner peace.

The remaining months before our divorce were rough. Thank God, I had the support of my family and good friends. The doubts, the tears and the lonely times that are a part of separation stayed with me. But, as time went on, I began to accept the fact that the marriage was over and I did my best to pick up the pieces and get on with my life.

Chapter 7

New Beginnings

Picking up the Pieces

AFTER SEVERAL MONTHS of living with my parents, it was time for me to find a place for Rob and me to live. Since Dave and Debbie had recently married, they were also looking for a place of their own. Dave found a row house that had been remolded and was two apartments.

The house could be owned outright rather than renting it on a monthly basis. It was actually cheaper than renting a complex. To make the monthly payments on the mortgage, Dave needed to rent out one of the apartments and it was perfect for Rob and I. Dave and Debbie wanted the downstairs apartment which was fine with me and Rob and me would not be alone.

One evening, as Rob and I sat in our sparsely finished apartment, I began to cry. All I ever wanted to be was a wife and mother. I knew I was blessed to have Rob, but I was having a hard time dealing with the fact that my marriage was over and I was still having nightmares due to the violence.

I would see happy couples and that would tear me apart. I know I was lucky in many ways; Rob and I were safe, we had a place to live and I had a job with my dad. But, it didn't change the fact that my marriage had failed and I felt like a failure.

There was nowhere to go but forward. Looking back only made me more upset. Unfortunately, the good times with Omar were overshadowed by the bad times. Cindy and Carol were there for me. The three of us were single moms each with a son to raise. On weekends we spent a lot of time together.

Even though we worked full time, it was a struggle to make ends meet. When we could afford to, we took our sons out for an occasional outing. Most weekends were spent at each other's apartment drinking endless cups of tea as the boys watched TV or played outside.

Our similar situation, interests and values brought us together. A deep, lasting friendship began.

The Divorce

OMAR HAD ACCEPTED the fact that it was over between us and it was time to move on. After a year and a half, Omar signed the divorce papers. The date was set for us to meet with our lawyers to appear before a judge to finalize our divorce and settle the dispute over custody and the return of all my personal belongings.

Omar had his own apartment and wanted more time with Rob. The fact that Omar had been abusive was overlooked. The judge granted Omar and entire weekend twice a month as well as one evening a week plus two weeks in the summer.

Visitations on holidays would alternate. I was disappointed my lawyer had not addressed my request for supervised overnight supervision by a family member of his until Rob was older.

There was talk of collusion between the lawyers but the judge let it slide as if it hadn't mattered. Mrs. Prodey, who had gone with me for support, was not happy with the judge.

Omar's request for joint custody was denied, a fact that was important to me. As far as my possessions, Omar argued that they had been returned when in fact they weren't.

That evening as Rob and I were alone in our sparsely furnished apartment, I began to cry. All I had ever wanted to be was a wife and mother. I knew I was blessed to have Rob, but I was having a hard time dealing with the fact that my marriage was over and I felt like a failure.

Rob was on the floor playing with his little truck when he looked up and saw me crying. "Don't cry mommy, you still have me!" he said

I looked at my beautiful son and opened my arms, inviting him to come over and sit in my lap. He ran over and plopped in my lap. I hugged him and replied. "you're right, I still have you, don't I?" I held him close for awhile until I stopped crying and began tickling him until we were both laughing.

Rob was already my "little man", offering support. I knew then, that unless I looked at things differently, I would not move forward. I told myself that I had to be stronger for Rob. It wasn't just me that was affected by the divorce.

Violet Sky

MY RELATIONSHIP WITH Omar had started off as a fairy tale romance. We met and fell in love under the Paris lights. He was affectionate and caring, always the gentleman. Then everything changed.

It had already been a year since the divorce and I still had issues to deal with, but I had come a long way. I was alone and afraid to get involved in a relationship. Although I would have loved to meet a man who cared about me and I could feel comfortable around him. I had a difficult time moving forward and I needed something positive to happen in my life. How do you emerge from the ashes?

The love I had for Rob kept me focused on being the best mom I could be at the time. His love often distracted me from feeling sorry for myself. I was lucky to have such a happy and loving little guy like Rob.

My faith had always kept me going in difficult times in my life and I needed to feel close to Christ again. Hurt and confused, I had backed away from Him.

My faith had been strong when I had heard the voice in Paris, I felt His presence in Beirut, I saw the vision and with the immigration process, my faith gave me the determination to finish what I had started.Even though I had grown weary during the abuse, I always believed Jesus was there with me, keeping me strong enough to take it when Omar exercised his free will to control his wife.

I knew I was going to be ok. I loved life and many of the people in it. I could still appreciate the simpler things in life; the smell of flowers after the rain, the unexpected hugs, a good cup of hot tea and at the end of the day, the violet sky that appeared after the sun went down.

Changes of the Heart

MY MOM HAD encouraged me to join the senior choir at church. I needed to get involved with church again and the choir was a good place to start. My mom, as well as close family and a few of my former classmates, were in the choir.

Although the choir was an important part of the church service, in some ways, it was separate from the congregation. The members who had hurt and judged me were not in the choir. Most of the choir members had known me all my life. They knew the situation with the Farahs and were very supportive.

One Sunday before church, Sandra a fellow alto, asked me if I would like to go with her to the Billy Graham Crusade. Her husband, our vicar, had a church matter come up at the last minute and couldn't go.

There would be a bus leaving the church parking lot after the last service. Rob would be with Omar until late that evening and I was free all day. I had heard about the crusade but wasn't sure what to expect.

That morning we had been asked by our choir director if anyone was interested in joining the choir for the Baltimore Crusade. Before I knew it, we were off to hear Billy Graham. Someone I barely knew about.

Baltimore's Memorial Stadium quickly filled with people. It was the first service beginning a week long crusade. As the crowd began to settle down, I looked around and saw people of all ages and walks of life who had come to hear Reverend Graham's message.

As Billy Graham talked about relationships I knew I had to let go of the bitter feelings I felt towards Omar to move forward in my life. I had to forgive him. Things happened and I could only change myself and my attitude. Letting go of the past was not easy but I had to get over it.

For the rest of the week I went every night. I either went alone or with a friend. Billy Graham and his guest speakers made a big impression on me. The crusade helped me change my life. I still look back on that week as one of the most inspiring weeks of my life.

Moving On

TIME MARCHED ON and Omar was moving on with his life while I was still having difficulty dealing with the fact that I was a single parent.

Omar was getting married and moving to Virginia. Robert had bought a bakery for the family to run, so everyone was moving out of Baltimore.

Omar's other siblings had kept in touch with me occasionally. I knew that by moving that far away, any contact I had with them would be affected. Regardless of any feelings we had towards each other, this was a chance for them to move on as well.

When I passed their empty house, it was a constant reminder that the people I had loved and worked hard to bring over to America, were out of my life. I felt as if I had lost them all over again. The only way to move on was to let go of the past but it was difficult

One weekend after Rob had left for a long weekend visitation with Omar, I sat on the steps in the hallway that led up to our apartment and cried. It had been and emotional time when Rob left because he had cried saying he wanted to stay home with me.

Almost five, Rob felt more comfortable in familiar surroundings closer to home. His first visitation with his dad in Virginia had left Rob wanting to come home.

Dave walked up the steps and sat quietly until I had stopped crying. "You can't do this to yourself, crying is not going to change things. I wish I had the right words to say" he continued "but I hate to see you so upset. I know this has been hard for you but you have to find a way to deal with this."

Dave knew and understood me better than anyone else. When I was young, my job as a big sister was to watch over Dave and now he was watching over me. Over the years, Dave had become my friend confidant and my soul mate.

We went up to my apartment and talked for awhile until I felt better about my situation and life in general. Dave had a way of helping me through different situations in my life that helped me change my attitude to a more positive way of looking at things.

In time, visitations became less stressful for Rob and me. The time we spent together became quality time rather that just going through the days. Dave had helped me change my outlook on both my life and myself that gave me the confidence to move on.

Mark

CONQUERING MY FEARS about personal involvement was the hardest part as far as meeting someone and having a relationship. I knew there were good men out there but my fear was going to be the hardest part to overcome.

Bruce had a friend he wanted me to meet. Mark was stationed with Bruce and both were electricians and bikers. I reluctantly accepted his invitation to come up to Cape May to meet Mark. I drove up when Omar had Rob for the weekend.

Bruce and I drove to the softball field where Mark was pitching for his team. After the game we went over to meet him. It was obvious he was popular with his teammates. After talking to him for awhile, Mark told us he would be over Bruce's house after he showered and changed.

The weekend went well and we hit it off. The next weekend Mark and Bruce rode their bikes down to Baltimore. The following weekend, I drove up with Cindy and our courtship began.

Family was important to Mark and he liked children. I was anxious for Rob and Mark to meet one another. He and Rob got along well. They were comfortable around each other which was important to me. If I was to get serious about anyone, he had to accept the fact that I had a son and to like him as well.

Mark and I began seeing each other as often as possible. We had similar values, interests and beliefs. Both out lives evolved around family and friends. When we were in Cape May, we would ride his Harley along the waterfront, park the bike and spent hours sitting on the beach talking.

It wasn't long before I met his parents. I was nervous to meet them but they were so accepting of Rob and me. They made us feel very comfortable. At a family gathering we met the rest of his large family and I liked them. They were happy that Mark had met me and was happy.

Mark was an attractive man with curly brown hair and green eyes. With his tanned and freckled skin, I was not surprised to learn he was Irish. When I told Mrs. Prodey about Mark, she wanted to meet him. The first time they met, we went downtown to the Irish festival. She surprised Mark by buying him a beer saying "every Irish man likes his beer".

Mrs. Prodey and Mark got along well from the beginning and she gave me her approval. Mark was good with Rob and my family and friends liked him. Mark was endorsed by Bruce and that was good enough for me.

One beautiful evening Mark had taken me to a restaurant in Cape May for dinner. The restaurant was on the edge of the water. We had a window seat with a small table. The flickering candle danced in the slight breeze. I knew I was falling in love and I was scared. Mark was never anything but gentle, kind and affectionate to me. I still worried, "how could I be sure he was right for me?"

After several months of dating, Mark proposal and I accepted. Both our families were happy about the engagement.

Our wedding took place at my church surrounded by our family and friends. My dad walked me down the isle. As I walked towards Mark, I was hopeful for the future and thankful I was given another chance with love and marriage.

Chapter 8

Cape May

Cape May

CAPE MAY WAS a beautiful seaside town. Victorian houses lined the streets and life took on a slower pace. Off season, Cape May was small town America. Little shops and restaurants dotted the town. Many of the Victorian houses were bed and breakfast hotels offering afternoon teas, for a small fee, to anyone interested.

The small pedestrian mall had an assortment of unique shops. Candles, ceramics and candy were made and sold in their store. The French bakery created pastries and bread that was equivalent to those in Paris.

Cape May itself was an island connected by two bridges to Cape May County. Surrounded by the ocean on the east coast and the Delaware Bay on the west, it gave people the opportunity of seeing both a sunrise and a sunset, across the water.

Cape May consisted of locals, Coast Guard families, and in the summer months, tourist. Except for the tourists, Cape May was a quiet and quaint town.

The Coast Guard training center and base were by the beach. Cape May Point beach, had its own light house and Bruce and Mark were responsible for taking care of the maintenance of the light house and changing the large light. Although it was a popular tourist destination, the light house was not open to the public. But, when we had visitors, Mark would let them climb the stairs to the top to see the view.

One thing you could count on in the military was that things were always changing. People came and went due to transfers or getting out of the service. I made many friends while I was in Cape May, and I missed them terribly when they left. With every friend that moved away, another new friend would enter my life, although, one person does not replace another. Sadly I eventually lost contact with them.

Along with the many hellos and goodbyes, I am left with lots of good memories of many friends and the good times we had. It would be difficult to live anywhere that long without the good times to look back on.

The Ultimate Gift

MARK AND I weren't married for long when I realized I was pregnant with our first child. We were so excited but kept it to ourselves for awhile. Of course, Mark wanted a boy and I dreamed of a girl. After my pregnancy was confirmed, we told our family and friends.

A month later at 3 months, I began having cramps and spotting. After going to my doctor, I was told I should have complete bed rest. Rob was five and Mark was in Cape May, so it wasn't always possible. Mark's boss, Master Chief Adams, gave him emergency leave and he came down from Cape May.

A few days after seeing my doctor, I was having a lot of painful cramps and light bleeding and I remained in bed. After taking a long nap, only to wake up soaked in blood, I knew I lost the baby. Mark called the doctor and I was scheduled for a D & C the next day.

The pain and cramping after the procedure, was as bad as after birth pains, but emotionally, it was worse. I was devastated and inconsolable for days. I was worried I would not be able to have more children.

Several weeks later, we'd move to Cape May. Mark had found a house to rent off base until government housing was available. Moving away from my family and friends was hard for me and I was still depressed over my miscarriage.

From the beginning of our time together in Cape May, our house was often filled with friends; old and new, from near and far. My brother Bruce was often at our house with his two boys and often every weekend, we had friends and family visiting from Maryland and Delaware.

It became a joke that company had to book weekends in advance. They say if you build a pool in the yard, you have friends you didn't know you had. When you live at the beach, the family and friends you do have, visit often. At least twice a month, Mark would invite a friend over for dinner. Nothing like a home-cooked meal for a single guy stuck on base.

Mark was on a bowling team on Tuesdays and on Thursdays, I had my quilting classes with homework consisting of sewing several squares of different patterns for the next class. Quilting kept my mind occupied with material and patterns, rather than having a baby. I was glad for the distraction.

Three months after moving to Cape May, I realized I was pregnant. I said nothing to Mark until I was sure and the doctor had confirmed my pregnancy. We had kept the news to ourselves for awhile, but things were going well and we were both excited. Rob, however, was a bit nervous.

His father had told him if and when another baby arrives, he would not be as loved or wanted. When Mark and I found that out, we both talked to him and assured him we would always love him and let him know how important he would always be in our lives as our son and to the new baby, as a big brother.

A few months later, several of my friends from Baltimore, came up one Saturday and surprised me with a shower. Others had given us gifts for the baby and except for a crib, we were pretty much set. As far as what we needed. Our families were eager to help us out and set up a nursery with what we needed. Now it was just a matter of time.

Mark, Rob and I had spent a lot of time at the beach during the summer. Between our daily activities and our frequent company, time passed quickly. A few weeks before our baby's due date, our house on base was completed. With the help of friends, we moved into our new house. Many of the neighbors even either worked with Mark or he knew them.

For a few days before I went to the hospital, I had contractions that went on for several hours only to stop. It was two weeks past my due date, but the doctor assured us the baby was fine. The day finally arrived when I was in labor.

Mark called the doctor and he was to meet us at the hospital. Since my labor with Rob was long and I had been having false labor for two days, the doctor assumed this labor would also be a long one.

After being admitted to the hospital, I was walking down the hall when I suddenly burst out crying, surprising myself.

"Why are you crying? What's wrong?" The nurse asked, caringly. "I'm just so happy!" I cried.

After being in hard labor for an hour, the doctor arrived just in time. By the time I was ready to deliver he had to deliver the baby with his socks on, and my labor was shorter than he thought it would be.

Mark had planned to be at my side for the delivery but almost passed out and had to leave the room. He missed the delivery by minutes. After so many times of wondering why I had lost our first baby I only had to look at my beautiful Irish girl and I knew the answer.

The Truth Be Told

WHEN ROB WAS almost seven, he asked me why his dad and I got divorced. He was old enough now to know the truth, but I felt Omar should be the one to tell him. For a few years, he had asked me why we weren't together but, I wanted to wait until he was older and he could understand.

It was important to me that he would form his own opinion and relationship about and with his father before he knew the situation that caused the divorce.

One very snowy day in Cape May, my friend Carol and I were watching the snow come down heavily. Omar was going to pick Rob up for visitation and I worried about them driving down to Baltimore.

"Don't worry", Carol assured me, "he won't make it up here in all this snow." About an hour later, Omar was at the door to pick up Rob.

Over the years, Omar did not miss a visitation unless he or Rob was sick. He had proved to be a very devoted father and Rob loved him. Since Omar had him for the weekend and they would have plenty of time to talk, I told Rob to ask his dad about our relationship.

When Rob came home that weekend, he told me what his father had said. Omar had admitted that he had not been very nice to me and that he would get angry and hit me. He said he was sorry because I did not deserve to be treated like that. I was relieved to hear that Omar had told the truth about our marriage.

At the same time, I felt sorry for Rob to find out the truth. Rob felt bad after hearing what had happened between his dad and I and asked me if I had forgiven him, for what he did.

I admitted to Rob that it had been hard to forgive him and that it had taken me a long time to do so. I told Rob that anger only grows and makes you bitter unless you let it go.

Although I forgave Omar, I could not forget, because for me, remembering had made me realize I could not go back to him. Omar had denied it for so long.

I made sure that Rob knew that his dad and I did love each other and that at times we were happy. He was born because his parents had loved each other, even though love doesn't always work out the way we hope it will.

It has been said, a leopard doesn't change his spots, but I believe Omar did change. I wished it had been sooner.

Hurricane Gloria

OVERNIGHT, THE WINDS had increased, causing waves to break over the sea walls and flood the streets on the small coastal highway. The ocean was very choppy with white caps as far out as I could see. Foam had gathered at the water's edge making it look as though suds had formed due to soap in the ocean. Private piers in low-lying areas were becoming submerged by the excess water. Birds hoping to find fish in the choppy seas dove into the water to get their meal for the day.

For the past two days, almost everyone in Cape May had been checking with the Weather Channel as we watched hurricane Gloria move up the eastern coast. The hurricane had not lost its force as it moved north, so a full evacuation for all residents and coast guard personnel in Cape May had been issued. Only those who had duty or were stationed on a boat had to remain on the island.

The Coast Guard had sent bulletins out to all residents telling them how to prepare for a hurricane. Because of the strong wind and heavy rain fall, windows must be taped, everything outside secured and in the event of flooding, anything that could be moved upstairs, should be moved. After all precautions have been taken, residents were told to leave as quickly and calmly as possible. Unless Gloria suddenly changed her course, the hurricane would hit Cape May.

As other residents in our courtyard were hastily packing their cars to evacuate, the four of us were off to see my obstetrician. Already five days past my baby's due date, I was in the early stages of labor. Mark's chief had given him some time off because of my situation.

Never having experienced a hurricane before, I was both nervous and curious. So before the hurricane got any closer, I had talked Mark into driving me the short distance to the beach. Mark stayed in the car with the children while I viewed the ocean from the edge of the beach.

Even though the hurricane was miles away, the fury and power of the wind and the waves was incredible. It was rainy and cold. The spray from the ocean's waves whipped across my face so hard that it stung. In the distance, dark clouds were quickly moving in our direction. After a few minutes of seeing what looked like an angry sea, I headed back to the car.

After being examined by my doctor, we were told to find a motel near the hospital. The doctor strongly advised us to go to the hospital before the storm hit and stay there in case my baby was born during the time the hurricane hit Cape May. We could stay there until it had passed us by. Both my doctor's office and hospital were located in Cape May Courthouse, part of New Jersey's mainland.

Luckily, there was a vacancy at a motel around the corner from the hospital. Far enough inland, the hospital and the motel would be safe from the worst of the hurricane. Soon I would be dealing with two forces of nature; a hurricane and labor and I had a fear of both of them.

Before the hurricane hit, the four of us went to the hospital. Through the large glass window, I could see that the wind had picked up speed and caused newly fallen leaves and debris to blow in a circular motion across the parking lot.

After Mark and the children were settled in the lobby, I went upstairs to the maternity ward. When I walked over to the nurses' station, I was asked my name and one of the nurses came over from her desk to talk to me.

"Your doctor called me and told me to keep you here and let you rest until the storm passes us. He also wants me to monitor your contractions. At least here you know that your family will be safe and if anything should happen, you're already here", she said as she began to lead me down the hall to my room. Several hours later the worst of the storm passed and the nurse came in to let me go.

"With the regular contractions you've been having, we will probably see you in a few hours", she warned, smiling at me. I went down to the lobby to join my family and head back to the motel.

Even though the eye of the storm had passed us by, we still had to deal with the wind of the storm, and from the lobby window. I could see that the gusty wind was still blowing debris around outside.

When we arrived at our motel, we walked up the stairs to our second floor motel room. I was afraid Rob and especially Katie would be blown away by the wind even though Mark had a strong grip on both of them.

We stood on the balcony for a minute and watched the trees bend to the point that we thought they would either snap or be yanked out of the ground because of the fierce wind. It seemed to me that the wind alone could cause severe damage with its strength. When the wind finally died down, we decided to take a drive to check on our house and get pizza.

Before the hurricane had hit Cape May, the wind had changed direction enough to have lessened the storm's impact on the Jersey Coast. For that, everyone was thankful. Damages were less than it could have been. Flooding appeared to be the biggest problem that we would see, but then, we hadn't seen the coastline or Cape May yet.

The one entrance to Cape May was blocked allowing only local residents on the island. Even then we were allowed to stay only long enough to check our house. Mark parked the car as he made his way through the flooded street to our house.

"Everything seems to be okay. The phone was working, so I called our parents to let them know that we were fine", he said as he rolled down his wet pants legs.

Except for a handful of other residents checking on their homes, Cape May was deserted. Before we left to head back to the motel, we drove around to see what, if any, damage had been caused by the storm.

Porches, steps and shutters had been ripped off houses by the fierce wind. Anything that hadn't been taken in or anchored to the ground had been hurled across yards and streets causing damage.

Boats from a small marina off a nearby inlet were strewn on the land due to rough water. Many of them were nearly destroyed with damage caused by them crashing into each other.

Flooding had turned streets into small rivers. The wind caused ripples across the water making the air feel colder than a late September day. We stopped at the pizza carry out before going back to the motel and settled down to await the birth of my baby.

As I relaxed and ate a piece of pizza, I began to have contractions. Once they became regular, I knew it was only a matter of time and we were off to the hospital again. After signing me in, Mark took Rob and Katie to stay with a friend who had duty. He came back to the hospital just as our son Johnny was born.

For the next few hours, everyone said the same thing, "too bad it wasn't a girl, you could have named her Gloria." Mark and I, on the other hand, were thrilled it was a beautiful, healthy boy. I quickly gave him the nickname "Hurricane Johnny."

Because of the hurricane, none of the new mothers had been released from the hospital, leaving room only in the halls. Later that day though, we had our own room. I had been thinking that because of the hurricane, no one would be around to stop in and visit me. But a short time later, I heard a familiar voice outside of my room. At first I thought that I had imagined it.

"Debbie! Lori! I don't believe it! Don't you know everyone's been evacuated?" I said half laughing, half crying. Debbie, her husband Tom, and their son had driven down from Buffalo, New York to meet up with Lori and Steve. From Allentown, PA the five of them then drove to Cape May to see the new baby.

The trip had been planned for a while but they had hoped I would have had the baby and been home already. They had not planned on a hurricane either, but they made it. After hugging and kissing them both, I told them I could never call them fair-weather friends.

The next day, my son and I were released from the hospital and went home. Before I settled into bed with my baby, I looked out the window that looked out into the backyard. Beyond our back fence was what looked like a huge pond where a lot of water had not yet worked its way into the ground.

On the pool of water were ducks, swimming and splashing around. Other birds alongside of it would stop to get a drink of water. The sun glistened on the water causing reflections to dance across the temporary pond. I had safely survived the hurricane and the delivery of my baby and I felt very lucky indeed.

My Sunshine

OFTEN, THE BEST things in life are not the planned, they just happen. I was surprised and excited when I realized I was pregnant. Rob was eight, Katie was just over two and Johnny was not quite one. I was a bit nervous about telling Mark but he was happy about my pregnancy.

My growing family kept me busy and I had been working at the commissary on base. Time had gone by quickly and I was already in my final month. I kept working until three days before my delivery. My doctor told me it wouldn't be long before my baby would be born.

When I went into labor, Mark called the doctor and we headed for the hospital. The doctor still hadn't arrived when I was about to deliver. The OB nurse who was with me was new. She had never helped deliver a baby; the closest she had come was to watch a delivery. After my water broke, the nurse began to panic and asked me what to do. The role was reversed and I had to tell her what to do.

"Just calm down and catch the baby". Thankfully, it was an easy delivery and my baby was born without any complications. My baby was born sunny side up and smiling. "It's a girl," the nurse cried.

Because the doctor still hadn't arrived the nurse wasn't sure how to cut the cord. She handed me the baby and covered us with a warm blanket. I was still having contractions because I hadn't delivered the afterbirth.

Finally, the doctor on call came into the room and cut the cord. After delivering the afterbirth, the nurse handed me my beautiful little girl.

The next day, my doctor and the nurse that assisted in the delivery, came into my room. I greeted the nurse with, "hi doc, you did a great job." I said nothing to my doctor until he asked me how I was doing.

Mark had been furious about the doctor's absence and went outside the room to talk to him. The doctor eventually came in following Mark and apologized. "We we lucky there were no complications," was all I could say to him in reply.

It was obvious by my tone that I was not happy with him either. The nurse was glowing with pride as word got out that she delivered a baby on her own and I was happy I had a healthy, happy baby that could brighten my day with just her smile.

Isolated Duty

MARK'S TIME OF being stationed in Cape May was almost up. Before Kim was born; he put in a request for four more years in Cape May. We were happy in Cape May and since my mom had been having serious medical problems, I didn't want to be too far from her.

After Kim was born, my mom came up to visit as soon as she had her doctor's permission after suffering another stroke which left her left arm temporarily paralyzed. But, she was still able to bake cookies with Katie and hold her new granddaughter.

During my Mom's visit, Mark received his orders. The only way he could be sure his request would be approved was to serve a year of "isolated duty" or take a change and not know where he would be stationed next.

A few days after my mom left, I called my parents to let them know that Mark would be going to Alaska for a year. The kids and I would stay in Cape May. We had some good friends on base and I would not feel as if I were on my own.

My dad called me back a few minutes after we finished talking. My mom was determined that the children and I moved to Baltimore for a year and live with them.

Although I said no because it would be too much for my parents, especially my mom, to have us all move in, she wouldn't take no for an answer. After talking to Mark about it, we decided it would be a good idea.

Mark had been worried about me being alone with four young children. Mark was given some time off to help us pack and move to Baltimore.

I would miss both living at the beach and my friends in Cape May. Life is full of hello's and goodbyes but little did I know then that going to Baltimore was about moving on and being where I needed to be.

Chapter 9

Baltimore

Moving to Baltimore

MY PARENTS WENT away for the weekend giving us the chance to settle in and move furniture. After the moving van left, there was furniture everywhere. Mark and Dave did their best to set up the bedrooms The rest of the furniture was scattered around the house.

Mark only had a few days left before it was time for him to go to Alaska. Except for Rob, the other children did not understand daddy would be gone for awhile. Mark told the kids he would call as often as possible so they could hear his voice.

A year would be a long time but, it was a lot easier for us than for families whose men went to war. The day had come for Mark to start his journey to Alaska. After an emotional farewell, Dave took Mark to the airport making things a lot easier for us.

Time seemed to go slowly at first but once the kids were settled into their new home and surroundings they quickly settled into a routine. My parents enjoyed having my children so close to them.

One evening, my dad came home from work as usual but was acting strangely. He was unsure of where he was and who he was. A few minutes later he would repeat the same questions. My mom, instead of panicking, replied lightly, "Bob you just asked me that." "I did? Am I Bob? Do I live here?"

He was sitting up in bed watching TV with my mom. For a few minutes he would watch the show and then ask her the same questions again. My mom called out family doctor who came over to see him. After knowing our doctor 25 years, he didn't recognize him. We saw Dr. O'Donnell almost every day.

Our dental office was on the ground floor of his house along with Dr. O'Donnell's offices. They talked while and Dr. O'Donnell asked him questions. My dad remembered enough to come home and feel at home. He knew where the coffee pot was, a good sign.

My father was diagnosed with "temporary amnesia". It happens when someone has so much on their mind or worrying too much. Even though I did what I could both around the house and helped out with my mom my dad had the bigger responsibility, his wife was dying.

Since we had moved in, the number of people in the house had gone from two people to eight, which only added to the stress. The doctor assured us he should be fine in the morning and to let him know how things were going.

When the doctor left, she explained the situation to my dad. It was almost comical to watch my parents. Everything was almost normal the way they interacted after 40+ years together.

My mom's health was getting worse and her cancer made her weak. Both my dad and I helped out as much as we could with caring for her. On a good day, my mom would get up and get dressed and potter around the house. She loved to cook and take care of her violets. Her mind was sound; it was her body that was giving out.

My dad's amnesia was up-setting me and I was scared. I went downstairs and cried. I had no idea what to do. I called my mother-in-law in Delaware and told her what was happening. I missed her son!

I told her that earlier I had prayed that God would take her soon so she didn't have to suffer more than she was. I didn't want my mom to die; I just wanted her to be relieved of her pain.

My mother-in-law understood what I meant and it made me feel better talking to her. I was grateful I was close to my in-laws. We had a mutual love and respect for each other.

As the evening wore on, my parents were still propped up in bed, watching Johnny Carson as usual. Both were laughing with him and the audience. My mom was happily crocheting and my father was having his coffee and dessert in bed.

They were going through their normal evening routine. My parents were laughing at Johnny as if nothing was wrong. My mother-in-law had helped me through a difficult night. Life was good.

A Death In the Family

MY MOM WAS sitting on her bed as she tied the bow of her blouse. She looked tired and sad. I sat down next to her and asked if she was okay. She didn't answer at first, but her eyes began to fill with tears. I gently put my arm around her and gave her a hug. She always tried to look her best, I thought to myself.

"I'll never get to wear that outfit you bought for me", she said.

"You'll be able to wear it in the fall weather too mom", I replied.

"No Karen, my cancer has spread", she said.

"Mom, you'll get better", I said trying to make both of us believe it. My stomach sank and I was afraid. I didn't know what to do or what to say.

"I never did get to write the book I always said I'd write", she said with a sigh.

"Well, then I'll write a book!" I said, determined to keep her dream alive. Then we both began to cry as we hugged one another. I had an eerie feeling she knew she was going to die soon.

For the next two weeks, my mom worked on canning tomatoes, tomato sauce, apricots and peaches. No one could slow her down even though her ankles swelled and she was growing very tired. It was as if she was determined to finish all she could.

It was Labor Day weekend and she was becoming impatient with the slightest things. The Jerry Lewis Telethon was on TV, so I took the children and my two nephews for a drive around the neighborhood collecting money for the telethon.

A few hours after collecting money, we dropped it off at the TV station. As we were leaving the station, one of the cameramen told us to go home because he had filmed them and they would see themselves on TV.

As soon as we got back to my parents' house, we went in my mom and dad's room to watch the kids on TV. When they showed the clip, my mom got the biggest kick out of it. She needed something to lift her spirits.

Very early the next morning, my dad called upstairs for me to wake up. There seemed to be something unusual about his voice and he was waiting for me at the bottom of the stairs. I followed him in silence until we were right outside my parents' room and then he stopped walking as he turned toward me.

"Mom died early this morning", he said as he began to cry. I had never seen my dad cry before. Speechless, I began to cry as I walked into their bedroom.

I walked over to my mom's lifeless body on the bed and gently held her hand in mine. I touched the soft skin on her face, whispered I love you and kissed her goodbye one last time. My life would never be the same again.

The Following Days

I HAD AN emergency number to reach Mark in Alaska, it was strictly enforced that it was just for emergency calls. Personal calls were permitted once a week when the men were allowed to call home.

Because of the time difference, it was in the middle of the night when I called Alaska. I was insistent that I needed to talk to Mark or his commanding office to let Mark know about my mom. A few minutes later, I was talking to his CO and I could not help but cry as I was talking to him.

Because of the situation, compassionate leave was granted to Mark. He was to be in Baltimore the next day. Before he left Alaska, Mark put in a request to be transferred to Curtis Bay in Baltimore instead of going back to Alaska. He had only served three months of isolated duty leaving him nine months of his enlistment. As happy as I was for Mark to be coming home, I was too upset to be excited.

The sad and ironic thing was that Bruce had recently been stationed in Curtis Bay for four years. He had been planning on leaving for New York in a week. Instead he was driving from Montauk for mom's funeral. Both Bruce and my mom were looking forward to his being home. We would all be together again in Baltimore.

I was a wreck that day. I cried continuously and had to take sedatives to calm down. Carol came over right after I had called her. She stayed with us all day. It was Labor day and she had been looking forward to having the day off.

Both my Dad and Dave were concerned I was taking it so hard and Dave thought getting out of the house for awhile would be a good idea. Dave and Carol drove to Dave's house with the kids and me.

It was Dave's idea to take the kids so Dad could have some time without the noise and confusion of the children. We were at Dave's long enough for them to watch a movie when Dad called. He wanted his grandchildren to come back to the house, without Mom there, it was too quiet.

Friends came and went during the day bringing casseroles, desserts and other dishes. Many stayed awhile keeping Dad company and offering comfort and support.

Everyone pitched in and helped with the children. Carol would hold Kim as well as feed and change her. Carol's kindness was so appreciated that day. Bruce and his wife arrived later that afternoon. The rest of the day remains a blur.

By noon the next day Mark had arrived. Dave and Bruce went to pick him up at the airport. I wasn't much better than the day before but his being home helped the children and gave me comfort by just being there. Johnny didn't understand why mommy was always crying and Katie was waiting for Grandma to come home. Rob had gone into my parents bedroom with my Dad after she died to say goodbye to her.

Earlier in the day, the pastor came over as we planned the memorial service with my Dad, brothers and me. All of us were too emotional to give a eulogy, but several close friends had offered to say some words,

The church was packed for Mom's funeral. She had meant a lot to many people. As her favorite hymns were being sung, I wondered how I was going to go on without her.

Getting on With Our Lives

THE DAYS AND weeks following my mom's death was like living in a fog. A day didn't go by that I didn't miss her. I had a hard time coming to terms with her death.

My brothers came over often and in getting together we grieved and drew strength from one another. Although we all wished the circumstances were different, my brothers and I were together again and close to our dad. It was fate that had brought Mark and me to Baltimore when we did.

My dad had a difficult time without mom and he could not have faced coming home to an empty house. Time marched on and each day was a bit easier to deal with.

Bruce and his wife moved into Rob and my apartment where Dave and his wife and their two sons lived. Bruce was now stationed in Cape May where Mark was also stationed to finish out his time with the Coast Guard but they worked in different areas. They enjoyed their time together off work more without seeing each other all day.

We got together often for cookouts and crab feasts.

Once a week I got together with my sisters-in-law working on crafts, watching a movie or just hanging out together. Our husbands got together on weekends for a ride on their bikes and a beer. On the weekends, the men would get together to ride their bikes or go for a beer, giving them the chance for a break, like we had during the week.

In the following months, Dave and Debbie moved into their own house and our dad had begun dating a widow my parents knew from church. We were glad to see that dad was happy. He had been a faithful husband and at 62 was young enough to be starting a new life.

A year after my mom had died, my dad remarried and moved out of the house leaving Mark and our family to live there on our own. We rearranged furniture making it feel more like our house rather than my parents' house.

Life was going well for all of us and our mom would have been glad to know that we were all together and moving forward with our lives.

The Spirit of Christmas

THE AROMA OF baked cookies and pies drifted through the house as the lights from the Christmas tree flickered across the living room walls. The Christmas carols playing on the stereo were like old friends encouraging me to feel the true giving and loving spirit of the season. As much as I didn't want to admit it, I felt as if I had lost the Christmas spirit.

Christmas hadn't been the same for me since my mom had died. That year seemed even harder without her than the year before. John and I were more worried about feeding our children than in playing Santa. Money was very tight that year.

It was Christmas Eve and my brother and I, along with our families, were invited over our dad and stepmother's apartment for an early dinner. Mark and I were already running late for the get-together when my dad called. He wanted to know when we would be coming over. I told him that we'd be there as soon as I finished wrapping the last of the cookie baskets.

When we arrived to their apartment, we were surprised that no one else was there yet. My dad had to leave to pick up one of my brothers and his family since their car had broken down.

We settled in and visited with my stepmother for awhile. A short time later, everyone arrived and we spent the next several hours visiting with each other before different schedules took us in different directions.

We all left the apartment about the same time. My dad and stepmother were going to her daughter's house. As we were leaving to get in our car, one of my brothers had invited all of us over to his house after the family service at church, for a gift exchange.

When we arrived at our house, Mark unlocked the door as I ushered the children in from the cold air. I was helping them with their coats when Mark noticed something was different.

"Someone has been in the house while we were gone," Mark said.

"How can you tell?" I asked as I took off my daughter's coat.

"There's a fruit basket on the table" he said, continuing his thought, someone must have left it here since we weren't home."

"No one just walks in your home if you're not there, they would have left it on the porch or something. Is there a card with it?" I asked, wondering who had left it.

"It says Merry Christmas, Santa", he replied after reading the card.

We opened it and found it was overflowing with grapefruit, apples, oranges, pears, bananas, assorted cheeses and nuts. At first we didn't notice the large basket beside the table that was filled with different kinds of cereal, macaroni and cheese, Kool-Aid, pretzels, tea bags and assorted boxes of crackers and cookies. It also contained a card which read, Merry Christmas, Santa. Mark and I gave each other questioning look, "Who could have done this?" we asked each other.

"Look at the tree!" Katie cried. "Santa has been here!"

Under our tree were presents for every one of us; each with a tag that read, Merry Christmas, Santa. Each present was wrapped in shiny, royal blue paper with white ribbons. The tree looked like a picture in a magazine. The once empty stockings that we had hung on a fireplace mantel were filled and overflowing with assorted candy and other surprises.

Footprints were leading from the fireplace to the tree making it appear as if Santa had come down the chimney. The children and I cried in delight. Even Mark had tears in his eyes.

As we looked at each other, Mark said, "I'm beginning to believe in Santa." The children were so thrilled and excited, we let them go through their stockings and open the gifts.

Mark and I couldn't figure out who could have done this for us. We decided it had to be someone who knew we would be gone and would have a key. Only my dad and brothers had an extra key. So, I called one of my brothers and told him about what had happened. He sounded very surprised, but said he knew nothing about it.

"Maybe we'll find something out later", I said to Mark as I hung up the phone, "we'll see if anyone uses blue paper."

Later that evening at Dave's house, I told everyone what had happened. No one seemed to know anything about it. Everyone acted surprised and said they were very excited that it had happened to us. As I told the story, I'd begin to cry.

A few days later, the truth came out. It had been my brothers and sister in-laws. One evening they had come up with the idea and a plan. After Mark, the kids and I arrived at my dad's apartment, my dad was to call my brother to tell him that he was leaving to pick them up "the signal" and my one brother would call the others. They all met at our house, then "Santa" went to work. Everyone had wanted to do something special for us that year and they did.

A week later, Mark's two sisters came down from Delaware with a car load of food. They brought boxes of hamburgers, hot dogs, chicken, meatballs, vegetables, and pasta dishes with sauce, rolls, desserts and some munchies. Because of everyone's generosity, our freezer and kitchen shelves were full.

For a brief time, I felt as if there was little I could ever do in return for everyone making our Christmas so wonderful. But then I realized that by giving to us, they had given something to themselves. It warmed their hearts as well as ours.

I know it is better to give than receive. But that year, it was better to receive, knowing it was given in love. They had showed me just when I needed it most, the true spirit of Christmas.

Megan—An Answered Prayer

O N MY THIRD visit to the hospital in 24 hours, I was examined and admitted to the hospital. My labor pains were inconsistent and the nurse told me to walk around the maternity ward. Mark walked with me, stopping when I had a strong contraction.

Ten months earlier, I had prayed for a baby. My life had a void, a desire for new life. Although I loved my children dearly, something was missing from my life. Maybe wanting another child was selfish, but I longed for a baby. Mark was content with four children and was careful we didn't have another one.

Walking around the maternity ward had made me tired but sped up the labor. We headed back to our birthing room. Mark had a nap as I read my magazine. I had never had a birthing room before, it was more like a hotel room than a labor/delivery room.

Nine months earlier, Mark and I were watching the movie, Full Metal Jacket. An invisible dam of memories burst and flooded over. Overcome with emotion, I cried throughout the movie.

The actor, Matthew Modine and the character he portrayed was Don to a T. The characters' story was not like Don's except that he served in Vietnam.

Seeing the actor, I thought about Don and his friends Dave and Paul. The four of us often went out for Chinese food and /or hamburgers and fries.

I had tried to put so many memories out of my mind, it was hard remembering their names. Dave was a married man who loved his tequila. He blamed that on his Mexican heritage. Paul was a good-looking ladies man.

An unlikely trio of friends, they were fun to be with. In many ways their different personalities complimented each other. They were funny, intelligent and interesting. Each of them had character of their own, but put together, they were characters. It felt odd to have their memories come back to me. I missed Don's caring ways.

Aside from the fact that the movie was sad, I cried for a long time afterwards. Sometimes remembering can be difficult. Mark was concerned I had become so upset. I told him about Don, Paul and Dave. He did his best to console me and we talked for a long time before going to bed. A week later, I had a feeling I was pregnant, something I kept to myself for awhile.

As the night became dawn, I was exhausted. My doctor, wanting me to have energy for the delivery, gave me some Pitosin to speed up the labor. Two hours later, they disconnected part of the "bed" for delivery. The baby' basinet was in clear view. The basinet was my focal point as I repeated " . . . and it came to pass . . ." over and over.

When I had broken the news of my pregnancy to Mark, he was not happy. Having recently gotten out of the Coast Guard, we had no insurance.

Because money was tight, we had four children and I would be 39 when the baby was born, both Mark and my dad thought I should consider an abortion. I was both disappointed and hurt by their attitude. They brought the subject up enough times that it put a damper on my pregnancy.

When I had an amniocentesis and the results were fine, I told them about it. I also said I would be having this baby and that I didn't want to hear any more negative comments that only upset me.

The doctor was checking on another patient when the nurse went to get him. The delivery went smoothly and I was soon holding a beautiful little girl. Outside the snow began to fall. As I looked at my baby, I thanked God for my answered prayer and felt peace and contentment.

Life in Baltimore

LIFE SEEMED TO move at a slower pace that spring. Almost summer, the warm breeze blew through the leaves fanning my face. The children were asleep so I had my morning tea on my front porch swing.

A few months after giving birth to Megan, I started experiencing post natal depression and the migraines I had became more frequent. The medications I was taking helped me, but it did not solve the problems.

There was little I could do to stop the headaches but as for the post natal depression, understanding the cause was a key to living with it. I was fortunate to have an understanding doctor who had also experienced it after the birth of her son.

My doctor told me that getting out in the garden had helped her. Spending quiet time when the children were sleeping was also important. She told me to make time for myself to relax, have a tea and clear my mind of any negative thoughts. And to stop feeling guilty. It was a medical condition, not lack of love for my family.

I took my doctor's advice and began to fix up my garden. It helped me to relax and take my mind off housework. My stress was released as I worked with the garden. The children began to help me with the gardening and they used a lot of their energy while doing so.

As the plants began to grow, the garden became a family project. Mark found he enjoyed it too. Megan watched us from her swing and Johnny played in the dirt as we created a fruitful garden.

Eventually, my depression went away. The front porch swing became a gathering place where we could relax and talk or read a book. In the mornings and evenings it was still a place where I could sit and just enjoy the tranquility.

Chapter 10

The Final Stories

Clutter in the Attic
Don and the Dream
The Phone Call
The Train Ride
The Gathering
The Victory Celebration
The Morning After
A Letter to a Friend
The Bakery
A Time for Reflection

Clutter in the Attic

THE HEADACHES THAT used to torment me on a frequent basis had become an every day occurrence. Instead of lasting a day or two, the headaches were present the entire day for weeks at a time. The pain would be so severe that at times, I could not move.

After years of office visits to different headache specialists, tests, an MRI, x-rays and different medications, I was told that I was fine, but it was confirmed that I had migraines.

While one friend took me to a healing service, others feeling they had the gift of healing, would pray over me. Nothing helped. The headaches were intense and I had reached my breaking point.

One day, a friend of mine told me about a woman who wanted to try and help me. A holistic healer, she believed in the healing of the entire self; mind, body and soul. Desperate for relief, I went to see her. We talked awhile about me and my headaches. Then we walked down the hall to the room where she worked on her healing.

We walked into a room in which she had a doctor's examination table in it. I was told to take my shoes off and get comfortable as she gave me a pillow for my head.

Before starting, she burnt some incense and put on a tape of harp music for a calming affect. I was told it would help clear my mind while she prayed for guidance and began "gathering her angels" as she called it.

"Are you ready to begin?" She asked quietly.

"What did you mean when you said you were gathering your angels?" I asked

"You believe in angels, don't you?"

"Well yes, but . . ."

Not letting me finish my thought, she replied "angels are always around us," she continued, "is there anyone close to you, who has died?"

"My mother passed away 20 years ago." I answered.

"Was there anyone else close to you who have died?"

"My mom had given birth to twins, a boy and a girl, but they lived less than a week," I replied.

"So you lost a brother and a sister?" she asked.

"Yes" I said.

"How about friends? She questioned again.

"I lost some friends in Vietnam", I stated matter-of-factly.

"Anyone especially close?" she continued.

"Don" I quickly replied.

Like a prayer, she asked that those I mentioned would be with us in spirit.

As I lay on the table, I was asked to relax enough for her to move my arms without me helping, just like a limp doll. When she felt my body relax, she began to touch different parts of my body.

This was done so she could draw different memories from my body. I would remember an experience from my past, and if the memory was a painful one, I was told to release it and let it go. She said the memories would remain, but any pain accompanying them, would be gone.

By the tenseness in my body, she told me I was carrying around too much "clutter in the attic."

At first, I felt a sense of peace. After I had left her house; but over the next few days, old memories would suddenly come back to me. I became obsessed with the different memories playing in my mind and I couldn't turn them off. I was afraid I was going crazy. As quickly as the memories came, they left.

On my next visit with her, she told me that by the releasing of old experiences and remembering different people and feelings, my healing could begin. Hopefully, I would put the past behind me and just deal with the present.

Don and the Dream

HE COMES TO me in my dreams, sometimes. Happy, full of life and no matter how much older I've gotten, we are still young. The dreams seemed so real, I would miss him when I woke up.

Don had been my kindred spirit his being 21 to my 18 years, he was someone I had looked up to. We were very close. I honestly believe he is one of my guardian angels.

A few days after seeing the holistic healer, I had another dream about Don.

As I opened the door, reporters began to take my picture. I was walking into a large, elegant hall, with a long chandelier lit corridor. The corridor was lined with doors leading to different rooms.

One reporter approached me and asked about my years as a USO hostess. He asked me to tell him about some of my experiences and people I had met. Don was the first person I had thought of. The next thing I knew, Don was standing next to me, smiling. I introduced Don to the reporter and we began walking down the long corridor.

Behind each door were different experiences and events in my life as a USO hostess. Every situation seemed so real and I recognized different people. I felt as if it was all happening again. The scenes flashed through my mind, one by one, until I came to the final door at the end of the hall.

The door opened into a beautiful, banquet hall with large windows surrounding the three sides of the room, making it a circular shape. Don and I walked into the room suddenly filled with people. Everyone was dressed in formal attire. Don and I walked outside to have a minute alone. I felt very happy and loved. Then I woke up.

The dream was so intense in the way it made me feel, that I sensed his presence with me. I got out of bed to try and shake the feeling.

My husband had already left for work and my children were still sleeping, so I had some time to myself. I walked into the kitchen to make some tea. Everything was quiet, but I had the feeling that I wasn't alone, as if someone was watching me.

I popped a Steve Wariner tape in the tape player to try and get my mind off the feeling. But the feeling of being watched, yet loved and protected, remained. I started to put dishes away when something seemed eerie. I stopped what I was doing and called out to him.

"Don? Don?, is it you? I feel your presence! If it is you, wrap your love around me for awhile."

The feeling of intense love and not being alone stayed with me for a while and then it was gone. I felt alone again. Throughout the day, all I thought of was the dream and of going to the Wall. After years of wanting to go there, it seemed unlikely I'd get there anytime soon.

The Phone Call

THE NEXT DAY the phone rang just as Rob and I were leaving for his guitar lesson. A few minutes later, I went to tell Rob we had to leave or we would be late. I looked at Rob and saw his eyes were full of tears, then he handed me the phone.

Omar had called to tell us that his brother Robert had died in Paris after a long battle with AIDS. During open-heart surgery, Robert had received some tainted blood and developed AIDS from a transfusion. Robert was neither gay nor a drug user. Although he had been sick for a while, it was still a shock. He was only 39.

Knowing Omar would want Rob to be with him and the rest of the family, I told Omar I would make arrangements to bring Rob down to Virginia. Rob wanted me to go with him, so I talked to Mark and then made arrangements for us to take a train to Virginia.

While I was making train reservations, the ticket agent told me there would be a short stop in Washington, DC. The ticket agent reminded me it was the weekend of the victory celebration for those who served in the Gulf War.

After all the arrangements for the trip had been made, Rob and I went out for some ice cream and talk. We spoke of Robert. Both of us had shared different experiences with Robert that we talked about. At times we laughed, while other times we cried. Robert had been a good uncle to Rob and had helped me out more than once.

We talked about the Farahs and how so many things had happened since I had seen them. Omar and I had become more comfortable with each other and our situation. The hardest part for me would be seeing the family again. Over the years, the Farahs and I had seen each other on occasion, but not since the divorce had I seen them all together.

Not wanting to dwell on Robert's death any longer, I changed the subject and told Rob about my dream. I mentioned how I wanted to see the Vietnam Memorial and how maybe we could stop in DC on the way home. This trip might just be my chance.

The Train Ride

MY BROTHER PHIL, dropped Rob and me all off at the train station saving Mark the trip with our other children. The train station was full of people and excitement. Everyone was wearing either a patriotic shirt, wearing red, white and blue clothes or carrying small flags. Some people were handing out yellow ribbons to everyone.

That evening was the big fireworks display by the reflecting pool. During the day, parades and various activities had been planned and D.C. expected large crowds of people. Even though I had no plans to attend the events in Washington that day, the crowd's enthusiasm was contagious.

Cars had been added to the train because of all the people going to Washington. There were so many people on the train's platform, it was hard to get away from the crowd and find our car. So, we got on the nearest car to us.

I sat back in my seat as Rob got up to get himself a snack and tea for me. Rob got caught up in the excitement of the crowd and the train ride. We both wished we were going to a celebration rather than joining his family in mourning.

The conductor came around to collect the tickets and told me that we had first-class tickets and should have been in the front of the train. I apologized and told him that we had gotten caught in the crowd and with so much commotion; we just wanted to find a seat. He laughed and said, "No problem, but you better change seats in Washington; the last ten cars are coming off the train. But don't run you'll have plenty of time."

When we arrived at the station, it was a mob scene. We had to push our way through the crowd. We found our car and settled in our correct seats. I felt sad that we wouldn't be in Washington because I still had a strong urge to go to the Wall. The rest of the train ride was quiet and I thought about Omar and his family. It had been so long.

The Gathering

WHEN THE TRAIN arrived at Alexandria station, Omar's wife, Susan, was there to pick Rob and me up. Fortunately, Susan and I got along which made things a lot easier. The family was going to meet at Robert's house. Even though Robert lived in Paris, he had bought this house for both his father to live in and for himself when he made his frequent visits to the States.

Omar greeted us warmly with a hug and a kiss as his father and brother Simon, headed for the door. They also greeted both of us affectionately and I was glad to know that they still cared about me. I visited with them for a while as Rob went upstairs to put our suitcases in the bedrooms.

A short time later, Omar's brother Maroon and his wife Nadia along with their two daughters, Ahlena and Karen, arrived at the house. We hugged and cried. Maroon and Nadia loved me as I loved them.

Over the years, I had thought of them often and had missed them. It had been too long. The girls had grown so much since I had last seen them that I hardly recognized them. Maroon turned to me and said, "You know Karen is named after you, don't you?"

"Oh yes, I remember, how could I ever forget that?" I answered.

Karen and I smiled at each other. As we were catching up with our lives, I showed them a picture of my children. Rob had kept them up to date on my growing family over the years. They were happy for me that I had remarried a good man and was blessed with beautiful children.

Omar and Susan had been cooking chicken and some Lebanese food while we were talking. We all gathered on the large porch where we ate. The weather was beautiful and I was happy to see everyone again.

The Farahs hugged me periodically during our visit and told me that they had missed me. They all saw to it that I had anything I wanted and I felt good knowing that regardless of my divorce and remarriage, they still cared for me.

It wasn't long before Maroon and I began to remember some of the times we had together in Beirut. His daughter Ahlena was fascinated by our stories and asked how they ever got to the States.

"Your aunt Karen brought us here", he said. Maroon told Ahlena about how I had worked with immigration to bring the whole family here.

"If she hadn't brought us here, we probably would have died in Beirut", he continued.

"Oh, what a great story, you should write a book about it. This story would make a great movie!" Ahlena said.

"Well, I have thought about it," I admitted.

"You should Karen and if you need any help, just let me know", added Maroon.

With that, Omar looked at his watch and told Susan we'd better hurry or we would be late.

"I hope you don't mind", Omar said as he turned to me, "but Susan has to work tonight at the Red Cross booth outside from where she works in Washington and I thought I would take you and Rob to see the fireworks."

I couldn't believe it! I would be going to D.C. after all! I asked Omar if I could go to the Vietnam Memorial and he said yes. After all, we'd be close to it and would have plenty of time to spare before the fireworks started. Finally, after all these years, I would visit the Wall.

Omar asked Karen if she would like to go with us to Washington and keep Rob company. Rob and Karen are only a few months apart in age and they always enjoyed each others' company.

Since Ahlena had plans for that evening and Nadia had to work the next day, I had to say goodbye to them. But Maroon would meet Rob and me at the bakery the next day.

The Victory Celebration

CROWDED AS WASHINGTON was, it was a good thing we had a parking space reserved for us at the Red Cross building. The building wasn't far from where we wanted to go. As we got out of the car, Omar grabbed a large blanket to sit on for the fireworks.

Omar and Rob were talking, giving Susan and me a few minutes together.

"I have to say, you must have a calming effect on Omar, he seems so much more relaxed", I whispered.

She looked at me and smiled, "it was his heart attack."

Rob and Omar came over with a small American flag for me, which I waved periodically as we were walking down the street among the crowd. We walked Susan to the Red Cross booth and said goodbye. Then the four of us headed for the Vietnam Memorial.

Don and several other Vietnam vets were very much on my mind and it bothered me to see all the attention being paid to the soldiers involved in the Persian Gulf War, when the Vietnam vets had been given such a cold and ugly reception when they returned home. I had never really gotten over my anger from the reaction and treatment they had received. Maybe by going to the Wall, I could begin to really put it behind me.

There it was, the Wall. I had seen it so many times pictured in different magazine articles. Before I began to walk on the path along the monument, I touched the corner of it. I had only taken a few steps when tears began streaming down my face.

The tears continued the whole time I walked along the path. Rob had turned to ask me something, but Omar, noticing how upset I was, quickly ushered Rob and Karen ahead of me as he lead them along the Wall, giving me some time to myself.

As hard as I tried, I couldn't stop my tears, so I let them flow. It was too crowded to try and look for anyone's name engraved on the black, granite monument. Someone had placed a can of Budweiser and a few Slim Jim's in a see-through baggy and even through my tears, I had to smile at that.

When I had reached the end of the Memorial, I walked away from the crowd to cry alone and pull myself together. I hadn't cried that hard since my mom had died. I looked up and saw Omar, with Rob and Karen, waiting for me a few yards away. I took a couple of deep breaths to try and pull myself together, but I was still visibly upset. I walked over towards them and said nothing but "thanks" for a while.

Not far from the Vietnam Memorial, on the street, they were selling different T-shirts. One shirt caught my eye. On it were two different soldiers. The T-shirts said Vietnam-You Are Not Forgotten. "All right", I said aloud as I admired the shirt.

One of the soldiers on the T-shirt wore a helmet, but there was something haunting about it and for that reason alone, I didn't buy it. I wish I had. Instead, I got one about the Victory Celebration.

People were packed everywhere on the grounds of Washington on chairs, blankets, or just sitting on their jackets. I followed Omar as he led us close to the front of the crowd. Surprisingly enough, there was still enough space in the front, so we laid down the large blanket. Rob nestled between Omar and me.

"It's nice to have both of my parents together and be out somewhere", he said smiling.

"I'll bet it is", I said feeling sorry for him, so enjoy it for an evening."

Omar wanted to the get something to drink, so he took Rob and went to a nearby snack stand.

Next to our blanket was a man about my age, who said aloud, "no one ever went through all of this for us when we came home from 'Nam."

I almost said something to him, but a couple next to us said something to him. The guy next to us was also a Vietnam veteran, but he didn't sound bitter like the other guy. The two vets started talking and soon the three of them sat together and quietly swapped stories. I was glad the man had found someone he could relate to, instead of sitting there alone.

A decorated veteran of the Gulf War sat down close to the front of us. He was obviously with his parents and girlfriend. I began to think about him. Like the Vietnam veterans, he went off to war and put his life on the line for his country. Veterans in that war were killed and injured.

No war can be an easy experience to go through and I was ashamed of my attitude toward the men and women who served in the Gulf War. It had been a different war for different reasons and with different circumstances.

America learned by mistakes made in how we had treated those who served in Vietnam. We needed this time to come together as a nation and unite in this time of victory and the end of yet another war.

Karen began asking questions about Vietnam and told me what she had learned about it in school. Karen also wanted to know more about Beirut and the war, so we talked about it for awhile.

It was good talking to Karen. She was a sweet and pretty girl and I couldn't help but feel a little proud that she shared my name. It was good to have a chance to talk.

The lines for snacks were long, but soon Omar and Rob returned with a tea and snickers for me and whatever anyone else wanted.

As I gratefully took my tea and thanked Omar, I relaxed next to Rob as he sat between Omar and me. Karen sat lengthwise on the blanket facing us as we talked. Before we knew it, it had gotten dark enough for the fireworks to start.

The fireworks were nothing short of spectacular. New fireworks in the shape of stars, yellow ribbons and stripes with streamers, were added to the beautiful display. The crowd would ooh and ahhh and applause, as if on cue, together. Together, the country and the crowd were celebrating this war's end. I felt good, better than I had in a long time. As if by going to the Wall and this victory celebration, I had come to terms with so many things from my past. Not only Vietnam, but also with Rob's family.

When the fireworks were over, we walked back to the car. Susan was waiting for us and gave all of us a Red Cross T-shirt referring to Desert Storm. It had been a long, emotional, day and I was looking forward to going back to the house and going to bed.

In the middle of the night, I woke up. My arm was numb from sleeping on it. I sat up in bed until my arm and hand felt normal again. In my mind, I began writing a letter to Don about that evening and my dream about him that led me to go to the Wall.

How odd it was, I thought, to be thinking about writing a letter to a man who has been dead for over 20 years. I guess I've never wanted to admit how much his death had affected me.

The Morning After

THE SUN SHONE brightly as it filtered through the blinds. Looking around the room, I noticed how beautifully decorated it was. Robert had spared no expense when it came to decorating. The furniture was elegant and the curtains, the bed sheets and coverlet, down to the plush rug, had a designers touch.

The air from the window was warm and I just lay there in my bed thinking about Robert and how hard he had worked for all this. And now he was gone.

I got dressed to have breakfast with Rob and his grandfather. We talked for a while mixing English with Lebanese. His grandfather made us feel comfortable and he made me some Arabic coffee.

I couldn't help but think back to the time we had in Lebanon. He had once said to me, "I hope you don't marry my son, take him to America and leave him."

I did marry him, come to the states, put up with his behavior, bring his family here, put up with continued abuse and yes, then being put in a situation I couldn't live with, I had to leave him.

But, as if he could read my mind, he told me how much he missed me and how important his grandson, Rob was to him. He had made it clear to Rob and I that no-one would take our place in his heart.

Soon Omar came over and he and Rob went up to Robert's bedroom to begin the process of going through Robert's things. Pierre by then had arrived and as we were talking, Rob came downstairs with some wedding pictures of Omar and me, that he had found in Robert's night stand. Surprised that Robert had kept them all this time, Pierre, Rob and me looked through them.

"I can't believe he kept these", I said, amazed I was looking at them. "I always felt he didn't approve of me."

"He loved you for what you did to bring us here. He admired you", Pierre said. "We all love you", he continued.

His father nodded his head in agreement. I probably would have begun to cry had it not been for Omar coming down and telling us to get ready for the bakery. Omar's timing was perfect.

A Letter to a Friend

D EAR DON,

Just the other night I had a dream about you. In my dream, I was being interviewed about my years as a USO hostess. The man wanted to know about some of my experiences as a hostess and the people I had met there. You were the first person I thought of.

I told the man that you loved life; you were funny and very caring. Of all the people I have met in my life, you had the best outlook on life and death of anyone I have ever known. As a Christian, you looked at death as a beginning and not as an end. Many times I think about the things you had said to me. A day didn't go by while you were in Baltimore that either you didn't see me or call me. You were my best friend.

When I heard about your death, I was at the USO. At first I thought it was a cruel joke. All too soon, I learned it was true. I was consoled to hear you died quickly and with your friend's at your side. Some of the guys at the club helped me deal with your death and the death of your friends.

Life and the war continued, others went to Vietnam and others came back. I had to try to put your death behind me, but believing as you did about heaven, I knew where you were and took comfort in that.

Yesterday, I went to Washington, DC. to see a big, fireworks display. There was a victory celebration for the soldiers in another war in the Persian Gulf. For the first time, I visited the Vietnam Memorial. They call it "the Wall."

The Wall is a long memorial; a black, reflecting, granite wall with a path leading alongside of it. The names of those who were killed in Vietnam or as a result of the war, along with the names of those who are still missing, are engraved on it.

I had only taken a few steps on the path along the Wall, when tears began to stream down my face; they continued the whole time I walked along the monument. By the time I reached the end of the path, I had to cry alone and pulled myself together. So many people were there that I couldn't stop to find your name, but I thought of you and some other men I knew who had also lost their lives in Vietnam.

Along the monument, people left pictures, flowers or personal items. Someone had left a can of Bud with a few Slim Jims in a plastic bag. I thought of you.

The ones who had survived the war have had it hard. It has taken years to heal from the pain and memories caused by the war. Too many came back from Vietnam needing understanding or a good friend to turn to, and too many vets didn't get what they needed.

Not far from the memorial, they were selling T-shirts and one of them said "Vietnam-you are not forgotten." You and others who served there, were never forgotten, Don. No one who ever cared about someone who served in 'Nam will ever forget the ones they loved.

I miss you,
Karen

P.S. I am putting a copy of this letter in the middle of the Wall along with a rose and baby's breath. I'd like to think that somehow, you would get to read this.

Karen

The Bakery

AFTER OUR DIVORCE Robert had bought a bakery for the Farahs to make pita bread. They also made Pita sandwiches stuffed with mince meat, spinach and cheese and one, sandwich similar to a pizza but with Arabic spices without the sauce and cheese.

The Farahs would sell the bread and sandwiches at the bakery, but also delivered them to different stores and restaurants. Omar's brother Simon would be at the bakery today and then take Rob and me to the train station where he had a delivery to make. He had to be at the bakery the day before, so he wasn't at the gathering.

On the ride over to the bakery, Omar was telling us that his sister was flying in that afternoon from Paris with Robert's ashes. When Robert was in his final weeks, Sarah had flown over to take care of him. A small ceremony would be held in Baltimore at the cemetery where their mother had been buried. Robert's ashes would be buried next to her.

Maroon was waiting for us at the bakery and we all went inside. Behind the counter at the front of the store were some homemade pastries like baklava and other Arabic sweets and candy. It was also a small store for different Lebanese and Arabic items.

When we went inside by the machines that made the bread and pastries, I was surprised at how big the bakery was and how clean they kept all the machines and the area around them. Simon showed us just how all the different machines worked and what they made. While we were there, he made us some spinach and cheese sandwiches that I love.

Although it had started out as a family business, Maroon had pursued another job, but most of the Farahs worked there. They worked hard at the bakery and I was glad to see that they could set up a business and make it a success.

Before we left, Rob and I picked up some bastirma and olives from the deli along with some bread, sandwiches and baklava.

After talking for a little while, it was time to go with Simon as he had some deliveries to make on the way to Washington. We said our goodbyes to Mr. Farah, Maroon and Omar and left. As we rode to DC, Simon and I caught up with our lives since our last meeting.

Making good time with the deliveries, Simon had time to take me to the mall and get some flowers to go with the letter I had written to Don. I wasn't there long, but promised myself I would go back and find his name.

After Simon made his delivery to one of the food stands in the train station, Rob and I said our goodbyes to him and waited to catch a train back to Baltimore.

The Ride Home / A Time for Reflection

ROB AND I got some snacks and drinks for the hour-long train ride home and we settled in our seats. We talked about our weekend Things had gone better than I expected.

The weekend had given me the chance to put a lot of feelings behind me, I felt a lot better than I had in a long time. The trip had brought some closure to the Vietnam War and Don's death.

I had taken my "job" as a USO hostess very seriously and over the years as a hostess, I had become emotionally involved with the Vietnam War and the men who had served there, as well as the servicemen who were in the military serving our country in other ways and places.

My time in Beirut and being in a war zone had given me a better understanding of how difficult it was not only to fight in a war but also how difficult it was for the people who had to live through a war.

My time with Omar had opened the door to domestic violence and the difficulties of dealing with it and having the strength to get out of a bad situation so I could get on with my life and try to put it behind me and love again.

I was pleased that Omar, his family and I had gotten along, for Rob's sake too; it had given me the chance to heal some wounds.

As the train began its journey to Baltimore, I thought about my life and the people I had met who had both affected my life and from their stories had often inspired me. By being part of their lives, it had both changed and enriched my life.

I was surprised how many things from my past had come together and put an end to a lot of the pain from many different things that had occurred in my life. From that, I had learned acceptance in others as well as forgiveness.

I thought about the book I wanted to write about my experiences. I had emerged from the ashes of my past and had begun a new life. I looked forward to my future and the challenges and experiences my life would hold for me.

Summary about the Book

AFTER A VIETNAM War protest, Karen joins the Baltimore USO to support the troops.

On a trip to Paris, she meets Omar who changes her life. They visit his family in Beirut and are caught up in the horrors of war. They escape to Paris and marry before moving to America.

Through faith and determination, Karen brings Omar's family to America to escape the war.

Her marriage becomes violent and abusive and she leaves to rebuild her life and remarries. A dream and fate brings her past and present live together.

Her extraordinary stories, experiences and the diverse people she met, bring her story to life.